BANGIN' BEANS

60 Vibrant Vegan Meals Powered by
Plant-Based Protein

Bangin' Beans

SARAH DOIG

**Creator of
Sarah's Vegan Recipes**

PAGE STREET
PUBLISHING CO.

PAGE STREET
PUBLISHING CO.

Copyright © 2024 Sarah Doig
First published in 2024 by
Page Street Publishing Co.
27 Congress Street, Suite 1511
Salem, MA 01970
www.pagestreetpublishing.com

Distributed by Macmillan, sales in Canada by The Canadian Manda Group.

28 27 26 25 24   1 2 3 4 5

ISBN-13: 979-8-890-03023-8

Library of Congress Control Number: 2023945223

Edited by Sadie Hofmeester
Cover and book design by Laura Benton for Page Street Publishing Co.
Photography by Sarah Doig

Printed and bound in the United States of America

Dedication

To my amazing parents, for inspiring my love of food and cooking from a young age, encouraging me to pursue my passions and giving me the most incredible support and advice.

To my brother and sister, for your unwavering support, constant laughter and always believing in me.

To my husband, for accepting that our kitchen will be turned upside down on a daily basis, being the most supportive taste tester and making me believe in myself.

contents

Introduction 8

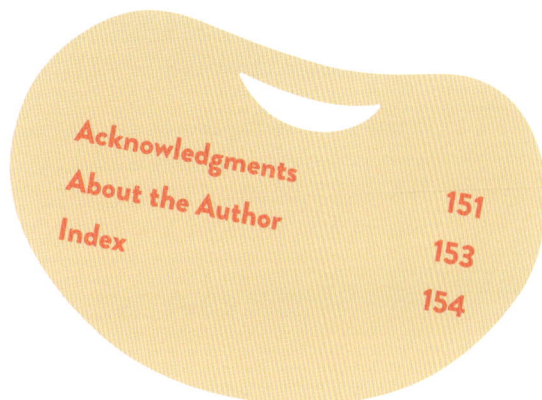

introduction

If you'd told me back when I was a four-year-old aspiring author, filling notepads with short stories, that one day I'd be writing the introduction to my first cookbook, I never would have believed you. But twenty-four years later, here we are!

Food has been a huge passion of mine from a young age: Both my parents love cooking. Growing up, we spent most of our time together in the kitchen. And many of my earliest memories are of eating and cooking with family.

Having always been a lover of vegetable-focused dishes, I decided to try out Veganuary in 2019. I spent the month of January eating plant-based and cooking up experimental vegan recipes. I quickly fell in love with all the new flavors and ingredients I was using, and with the way it was making me feel. So much so that after the month was up, I decided I wanted to keep going and permanently switch to a fully plant-based diet.

I began sharing snaps of my creations on Instagram, @sarahsveganrecipes, and joined the supportive community of vegan recipe creators. Fast-forward six months, I built my food blog, Sarah's Vegan Recipes (sarahsveganrecipes.com), to give my recipes a more permanent home on the internet.

My online following gradually started to grow, as did my determination to share vibrant vegan recipes that inspire and encourage others to eat more plants. There truly is no better feeling than when someone tries one of my recipes.

The idea for this book came about through my series of recipe videos, "Banging Beans." I love cooking with beans. They're affordable, packed with plant-based protein and fiber *and* they're extremely versatile. I was taken aback by how much my followers shared the same enthusiasm for bean-based recipes and really wanted to take it a step further. So here I am, sharing a collection of my best recipes featuring all kinds of hearty, delicious and nutritious beans.

Beans make such great vehicles for flavor and are a brilliant way to add protein to plant-based meals without breaking the bank. While all the recipes are, of course, vegan, this book is also targeted at those looking to add more plants to their diet and those searching for new plant-based dishes to add to their weekly meal rotation.

When developing the recipes, flavor was always at the forefront of my mind. You'll find a huge range of bean-based dishes in this book, covering everything from snacks and sides to cozy, comforting dishes, vibrant salads and everything in between. I want to show you that beans are so much more than just beans on toast! All the recipes in this book use canned beans for ease, but feel free to soak and cook dried beans if you prefer.

I really hope that you love the recipes as much as I do and that this cookbook becomes one that you find yourself reaching for often: when you're lacking dinner inspiration on a Tuesday night, when you have hungry family to feed in a hurry, when friends are coming round for dinner and when you want to try something new. Thank you for picking up this book. Happy cooking!

Sarah
x

SOUPS, STEWS & COZY BEANS

It's time to show beans the love they deserve! They're super affordable and an excellent way to pack plant-based protein (and fiber!) into your diet. Not to mention they're the perfect base for absorbing all kinds of flavor.

Whether you're looking for a warming bowl to snuggle up on the sofa with or a comforting meal to tuck into after a long day, these soups, stews and cozy beans will hopefully become regulars in your weekly meal rotation.

I've included some twists on classics, such as the Beany Minestrone (page 31) and Thai Green Coconut Beans (page 32), as well as combining exciting flavors and ingredients, such as the Spicy Peanut Butter Beans with Sweet Potato (page 24). The Creamy Lemon & Herb Beans (page 13) went viral on social media, and for good reason! They combine canned beans with simple ingredients and fresh herbs and lemon to create a deliciously creamy dish that's so tasty it'll have you eating it straight from the pot. All the dishes in this chapter can be eaten as they are, straight from the bowl as a lighter meal or served with some greens, roasted veggies, brown rice, flatbread or toasted sourdough alongside.

Creamy Lemon & Herb Beans

This is the dish I make whenever I can't decide what to have for dinner. It's my go-to comfort food and the meal I never get bored of. The ingredients are pretty straightforward and it's easy to make . . . but that doesn't mean it doesn't deliver on flavor! You can add some chopped greens—spinach and kale are my fave. Add them with the nutritional yeast and soymilk if you fancy; you might also need a splash more broth. For a tasty crunch, serve alongside toasted sourdough.

Serves 2 to 3

1 tbsp (15 ml) olive oil

2 medium leeks, roots removed and finely sliced

4 cloves garlic, minced or grated

1 (14-oz [400-g]) can butter beans, drained

1 (14-oz [400-g]) can cannellini beans, drained

Salt and pepper, to taste

5 tbsp (20 g) chopped fresh parsley, divided

¼ cup (15 g) chopped fresh dill, plus more to garnish

1¼ cups (300 ml) vegetable broth (stock)

3 tbsp (9 g) nutritional yeast

¾ cup (180 ml) unsweetened soymilk

Juice of 1 lemon

Zest of 1 lemon, to garnish

1 tsp chile flakes, to garnish

Heat the oil in a large pan over medium heat. Add the leeks and soften them for 5 minutes, then add the garlic. Stir for 1 minute to soften, then add the beans. Season generously with salt and pepper, and mix well. Mix in 3 tablespoons (12 g) of the parsley and all the dill.

Pour in the broth and bring to a simmer. Simmer for 5 minutes, or until the broth has reduced by half. Turn down the heat slightly and add the nutritional yeast and soymilk. Gently simmer over the heat until the sauce reduces to your desired thickness. Be careful not to boil, as the milk will split.

Stir in the lemon juice and season to taste with salt and pepper. Add the remaining 2 tablespoons (8 g) of parsley. Mix well and serve. Top with lemon zest, more dill and chile flakes.

Smoky chipotle Beans with zesty corn crema

The distinctively smoky flavor of chipotle livens up this warming black bean dish. I like using vegan beef broth for a deeper flavor, but vegetable broth (stock) works just as well. The zesty corn crema is a vibrant, plant-powered alternative to the classic crema or sour cream you might usually pair with spicy dishes, brightened with both lime zest and juice.

Serves 2

PINK PICKLED ONIONS
¼ red onion, finely sliced
2 tbsp (30 ml) apple cider vinegar

SMOKY CHIPOTLE BEANS
2 tsp (10 ml) neutral oil
1 medium red onion, finely diced
3 cloves garlic, minced
1 red bell pepper, finely diced
1 tbsp (15 g) chipotle paste or 1–2 tsp (1–2 g) chipotle chile (flakes or ground)
1 tsp smoked paprika
1 tsp ground cumin
1 (14-oz [400-g]) can black beans, undrained
¾ cup (180 ml) vegan beef or vegetable broth (stock)

To prepare the pickled onions: Add the onion to a small bowl and cover it with the vinegar. Set aside to pickle while you make the beans.

To make the beans: Add the oil to a large pan over medium heat. Add the onion and soften for a few minutes, until translucent. Add the garlic and stir over the heat for 1 minute, then add the bell pepper, chipotle paste, smoked paprika and cumin.

Sauté for 2 to 3 minutes, until the peppers soften. Add the black beans and their liquid. Mix well, then let it simmer for a minute before adding the broth.

Turn up the heat slightly and simmer for 5 minutes to reduce the liquid, stirring now and again to make sure nothing sticks.

(continued)

smoky chipotle beans with zesty corn crema (continued)

ZESTY CORN CREMA

1 cup (160 g) canned sweet corn, drained

1 tbsp (15 ml) fresh lime juice, plus more as needed

Zest of ½ lime

½ tsp apple cider vinegar

¼ tsp salt

¼ tsp garlic granules

1 tbsp (3 g) chopped fresh cilantro

1 tbsp (15 ml) fresh lime juice

TO SERVE

1 avocado, sliced

To make the crema: Add the corn, lime juice, lime zest, vinegar, salt, garlic granules and cilantro to a small blender. Alternatively, use an immersion blender. Blend until smooth. Season to taste with salt and/or lime juice.

Stir the lime juice through the beans just before serving. Serve the beans in bowls topped with the corn crema, sliced avocado and pickled onions.

pulled Eggplant & cannellini Bean stew

Slightly fragrant, spicy harissa pairs with smoky paprika, sweet cinnamon and earthy cumin to create a rich, flavorsome sauce. The cannellini beans add texture and protein while the eggplant is roasted until soft and silky and then pulled to give it an almost meaty texture. This flavor-packed, cozy stew is ready in less than an hour and is a firm favorite of mine through the colder months. Don't forget that garlic yogurt—it's cooling and creamy and perfectly complements the stew.

serves 2

EGGPLANT & BEAN STEW

2 small eggplants

3 tsp (15 ml) olive oil, divided

¼ tsp salt, plus more to taste, divided

1 medium yellow (brown) onion, finely sliced

3 cloves garlic, minced

3 tbsp (45 g) harissa

1 tbsp (15 g) tomato paste (puree)

1 tsp smoked paprika

1 tsp ground cumin

½ tsp ground cinnamon

1 (14-oz [400-g]) can cannellini beans, drained and rinsed

1 (14.5-oz [400-g]) can chopped tomatoes, with liquid

1 vegetable stock/bouillon cube

Black pepper, to taste

To make the stew: Preheat the oven to 425°F (220°C or gas mark 7). Line a baking tray with parchment paper.

Cut the eggplants in half lengthways. Brush the flesh with 1 teaspoon of the oil and sprinkle with ¼ teaspoon of salt. Place them flesh side down on the tray and roast for about 30 minutes, or until the eggplant is soft and silky and the skin is crispy. Remove the tray from the oven and leave to cool.

Add the remaining 2 teaspoons (10 ml) of oil to a large pan over medium heat. Add the onion and fry until soft and starting to turn golden, then add the garlic. After a couple of minutes, add the harissa, tomato paste, smoked paprika, cumin and cinnamon. Mix well. Add the beans and season with salt.

Once the roasted eggplant is cool enough to touch, use a fork to scoop out the flesh from the skin onto a chopping board. Use your fingers or the fork to pull it apart into strips. Cut any larger pieces into strips if necessary.

Add the pulled eggplant to the pan and mix well to let it absorb the flavors. Add the tomatoes and their juice, ⅔ cup (150 ml) of boiling water and crumble in the stock cube. Mix well. Leave to simmer and reduce for 10 minutes, stirring occasionally. Season to taste with salt and pepper.

(continued)

smoky pulled eggplant & cannellini Bean stew (continued)

GARLIC YOGURT

⅓ cup (85 g) plain, unsweetened vegan yogurt

1 clove garlic, minced or finely grated

¼ tsp salt

GARNISHES

Chopped fresh parsley

Flaked almonds, toasted

Meanwhile, make the garlic yogurt: Add the yogurt, garlic and salt to a small bowl and mix together.

Serve the stew topped with a generous dollop of garlic yogurt, some parsley and a scattering of flaked almonds.

creamy Tuscan Beans

These creamy Tuscan beans, aka "Marry Me Beans," are my spin on the crowd-pleasing dish commonly made with chicken. You definitely won't miss the meat here: hearty butter beans and cannellini beans are simmered in a luxurious flavorful sauce with garlic, oregano and sun-dried tomatoes. Some of the beans are blended with vegetable broth (stock) and the dish is finished with plant milk for a thick, creamy sauce with none of the dairy. Serve with garlic bread for the ultimate comfort dish.

serves 2

1 tbsp (15 ml) oil from a jar of sun-dried tomatoes

1 medium white onion, finely sliced

3 cloves garlic, finely chopped

⅔ cup (120 g) jarred sun-dried tomatoes, finely chopped

1 tsp dried oregano

1 (14-oz [400-g]) can butter beans, drained

1 (14-oz [400-g]) can cannellini beans, drained and divided

Salt and pepper, to taste

1¼ cups (300 ml) vegetable broth (stock)

2 tbsp (60 g) nutritional yeast

½ cup (120 ml) unsweetened soymilk

1 cup (30 g) spinach

Fresh lemon juice, to taste

1 tbsp (4 g) chopped fresh parsley

Add the oil to a large pan over medium heat. Add the onion and stir for a few minutes, until soft and translucent. Add the garlic, sun-dried tomatoes and oregano.

Stir over the heat for a couple more minutes, then add the butter beans and half of the drained cannellini beans (⅔ cup [125 g]). Season with salt and pepper and stir.

Using a cup blender or immersion blender, blend the remaining half of the cannellini beans (⅔ cup [125 g]) with the vegetable broth until smooth. Pour the mixture into the pan with the beans and mix well.

Turn down the heat slightly and add the nutritional yeast, soymilk and spinach. Stir over the heat until the spinach wilts and the sauce is warmed through. Squeeze in lemon juice to taste, and season well with salt and pepper. Serve in bowls topped with freshly ground black pepper and parsley.

Roasted Tomato & Butter Bean Soup

Tomato soup is a comfort food classic—this recipe takes it to the next level! Tomatoes are roasted for maximum flavor, then simmered with smoked paprika and chile flakes for warmth. It's all the best things: creamy, smoky, garlicky and a little bit spicy. Protein-packed butter beans add a little creaminess when blended, keeping it totally plant based. Grab a slice (or two) of toast and get slurping.

serves 3 to 4

3 cups (500 g) tomatoes, chopped into large chunks

4 cloves garlic, peeled

¼ tsp salt, plus more to taste

2 tsp (10 ml) olive oil

2 tbsp (30 g) tomato paste

1 tsp smoked paprika

1 tsp chile flakes

1 (14-oz [400-g]) can butter beans, drained and rinsed

Black pepper, to taste

2½ cups (600 ml) vegetable broth (stock)

1 tsp agave or sugar, to taste (optional)

OPTIONAL GARNISHES

Vegan cream or coconut cream

Chile flakes

Fresh basil leaves

Preheat the oven to 400°F (200°C or gas mark 6).

Spread the tomatoes and garlic on a baking tray and sprinkle with ¼ teaspoon of salt, plus more to taste. Drizzle with the oil. Roast for 15 to 20 minutes, or until the tomatoes are soft and blistered.

Add the roasted tomatoes, garlic and any juices from the tray to a large pot over medium heat. Add the tomato paste, smoked paprika and chile flakes. Stir to combine.

Add the beans and season well with salt and pepper. Stir over the heat for about 2 minutes, then pour in the vegetable broth.

Bring to a simmer, then simmer for 20 minutes further, until the broth has reduced by about one-third.

Blend until smooth. Add a pinch of sugar to taste, if desired, and season with salt and pepper. Serve in bowls and top with a drizzle of vegan cream, chile flakes and basil leaves, if using.

spicy peanut Butter Beans with sweet potato

Using peanuts in savory stews and curries is nothing new by any means—West African groundnut stew and Thai massaman curry are just two delicious examples. The ingredients in this dish are fairly straightforward, but the flavors are far from it. Black beans and sweet potato are simmered in a delicious sauce of creamy coconut milk, smooth peanut butter and fragrant aromatics. If you're a lover of spicy food, keep the seeds in the chile for an extra kick.

serves 4

2 tsp (10 ml) neutral oil

1 medium yellow (brown) onion, finely sliced

4 cloves garlic, minced

1½ tsp grated ginger

1 red chile, deseeded and finely diced

2 cups (300 g) sweet potato, peeled and cubed

2 (14-oz [400-g]) cans black beans, drained and rinsed

¼ cup (60 g) smooth peanut butter

3 tbsp (45 g) tomato paste

1 (14-oz [400-g]) can chopped tomatoes, with liquid

1 (14-oz [400-g]) can coconut milk

1 vegetable stock/bouillon cube

Salt and pepper, to taste

2 packed cups (60 g) chopped kale

Lime wedge, to serve

OPTIONAL GARNISHES
Roughly chopped peanuts
Sliced red chile
Fresh cilantro leaves

Add the oil to a large pan over medium heat. Add the onion and soften for 5 minutes, until translucent and starting to color on the edges. Add the garlic, ginger and chile to the pan with the onion. Stir over the heat for 2 to 3 minutes, until soft and fragrant.

Add the sweet potato to the pan and mix well. Add the black beans, peanut butter, tomato paste, tomatoes and coconut milk.

In a jug or mug, combine the stock cube with ½ cup (120 ml) of boiling water and add it to the pan. Mix well and bring to a simmer.

Simmer on low for 30 to 35 minutes, or until the liquid has reduced and the sweet potato is soft and cooked through. Season to taste with salt and pepper. Add the kale to the pan and stir through. Leave on the heat for a few minutes to let the kale wilt.

Serve in bowls with lime wedges on the side to squeeze over just before eating. Garnish with chopped peanuts, sliced red chile and fresh cilantro leaves, if desired.

Fragrant Black-Eyed Bean & Coconut Stew

Hearty, wholesome, cozy . . . this one checks all the boxes! Black-eyed beans and potato are simmered in a fragrant coconut milk broth flavored with earthy turmeric, warming ginger, citrusy cilantro (coriander) and green chile for a little bit of heat. Leafy kale brings a bright green contrast and extra plant points to the dish. On a cold evening, there's nothing better than a pan of this simmering away on the stovetop.

Serves 2

2 tsp (10 ml) neutral oil

1 medium red onion, finely sliced

2 cloves garlic, minced or finely grated

1 tsp minced ginger

1 green chile, finely diced

2 large tomatoes

1 tsp ground turmeric

½ tsp ground coriander

1 (14-oz [400-g]) can black-eyed beans, drained and rinsed

1 heaped cup (200 g) diced potato

½ tsp salt

1¾ cups (400 ml) vegetable broth (stock)

1 (14-oz [400-g]) can coconut milk

2 cups (50 g) chopped kale

1 tbsp (15 ml) fresh lime juice

TO SERVE

Chopped fresh cilantro

Lime wedges

Add the oil to a large pan over medium heat. Add the onion and sauté for a few minutes, until soft. Add the garlic, ginger, chile and tomatoes. Stir and then cook over the heat for a few minutes, until everything is softened and fragrant.

Add the turmeric, coriander, beans and potato. Add the salt and mix well. Add the broth and coconut milk and simmer for 30 minutes, or until the potatoes are fork-tender. Stir through the kale and simmer for a further 2 minutes, until soft and wilted.

Stir through the lime juice. Serve the stew in bowls, topped with a sprinkle of cilantro with lime wedges on the side.

Harissa Butter Beans with Tahini Yogurt Drizzle

This one-pot dish is ready in about 20 minutes, but it tastes like it's been simmering away for hours! The beans are cooked in a warming, smoky sauce with gentle heat from the harissa and subtle sweetness from the pepper and tomatoes. The tahini drizzle is the perfect accompaniment—it almost melts into the saucy beans, adding a cooling layer of creaminess.

serves 2

HARISSA BUTTER BEANS

1 tbsp (15 ml) olive oil

1 medium yellow (brown) onion, thinly sliced

1 red bell pepper, thinly sliced

4 cloves garlic, minced

1 tsp smoked paprika

1 (14-oz [400-g]) can butter beans, drained and rinsed

1 (14-oz [400-g]) can chickpeas, drained and rinsed

¼ cup (60 g) harissa paste

Salt and pepper, to taste

1 (14-oz [400-g]) can diced tomatoes, with liquid

¾ cup (180 ml) vegetable broth (stock)

TAHINI YOGURT DRIZZLE

½ cup (120 g) plain, unsweetened vegan yogurt

1 lemon, zest and juice

2 tbsp (30 ml) tahini

1 clove garlic, minced or finely grated

Salt and pepper, to taste

2 tbsp (8 g) chopped fresh parsley, to garnish

To make the beans: Heat the oil in a large pan over medium heat. Add the onion and soften for 2 to 3 minutes, until mostly translucent. Add the bell pepper, garlic and paprika to the onion and stir for 3 to 4 minutes, until soft.

Add the butter beans and chickpeas to the pan along with the harissa and a pinch of salt and pepper. Mix well, making sure everything is covered in harissa.

Pour in the tomatoes and vegetable broth and stir. Simmer over medium heat for about 15 minutes, stirring now and again, until the broth has reduced slightly. Season to taste.

Meanwhile, make the drizzle: Mix together the yogurt, lemon zest and juice, tahini and garlic. Season with a little salt and pepper to taste.

Serve the beans with a drizzle of tahini yogurt and garnish with the parsley.

Beany Minestrone

This is my take on a hearty Italian minestrone soup, and it's perfect to tuck into on a cold day. The tomato broth is deep with flavor, the chile gives a subtle heat and the two different types of beans along with the spaghetti make it wholesome and filling. Don't try to fast-track sautéing the veg—this is where the broth gets all of its flavor. I promise it's worth the time and patience!

serves 4

1 tbsp (15 ml) olive oil

1 medium carrot, finely diced

1 medium yellow (brown) onion, finely diced

2 ribs celery, finely diced

3 cloves garlic, finely diced or minced

2 tbsp (30 g) tomato paste

½ tsp chile flakes

1 (14-oz [400-g]) can borlotti beans, drained

1 (14-oz [400-g]) can cannellini beans, drained

Salt and pepper, to taste

1 (14-oz [400-g]) can chopped tomatoes, with liquid

4 cups (1 L) vegetable broth (stock), divided

1 oz (25 g) spaghetti

3 packed cups (90 g) shredded kale or Tuscan kale

TO SERVE

Extra virgin olive oil

Chopped fresh parsley

Chile flakes

Freshly ground black pepper

Heat the oil in a large pot over medium-low heat. Add the carrot, onion, celery and garlic and sauté for 10 minutes over medium-low heat, until soft.

Add the tomato paste, chile flakes and beans (drained but not rinsed). Season to taste with salt and pepper, and mix well.

Add the chopped tomatoes and 3 cups (700 ml) of the broth. Bring to a boil, then simmer for 15 minutes to reduce.

Crumble the spaghetti into pieces about 1 inch (2.5 cm) long and add to the pot. Add the remaining cup (300 ml) of broth and continue to simmer for 10 to 15 minutes. Once the pasta is almost al dente, add the kale and stir through.

Once the pasta is al dente and the kale has wilted, season to taste with salt and pepper and serve in bowls. Drizzle with oil and garnish with parsley, chile flakes and black pepper.

Thai Green Coconut Beans

Inspired by the vibrant ingredients and flavors of Thai green curry, this dish is light and fragrant but comforting at the same time. Cooking the eggplant and beans with the Thai green curry paste allows all the punchy flavor to be soaked up while the coconut milk makes the sauce extra creamy, lifted by a hit of fresh lime juice just before serving. Some Thai green curry pastes are not vegan due to the inclusion of fish paste, so be sure to double-check!

serves 2

3 cups (225 g) baby or Thai eggplant

2 tsp (10 ml) neutral oil

3 tbsp (45 g) vegan Thai green curry paste, divided

1 (14-oz [400-g]) can butter beans, drained and rinsed

1 (14-oz [400-g]) can coconut milk

1 tsp tamari or light soy sauce, plus more to taste

1 cup (50 g) Romano pepper, sliced into thin strips

1 cup (90 g) baby corn, halved or quartered

1 cup (40 g) snow peas (mange-tout)

1 tbsp (15 ml) fresh lime juice

Chopped fresh cilantro (coriander), for garnish

Lime wedges, to serve

Cut the eggplant into 1-inch (2.5-cm) chunks. Heat the oil in a medium-sized pan over medium heat. Add 1 tablespoon (15 g) of the Thai green curry paste and fry over medium heat for 5 minutes, until the eggplant is soft.

Add the remaining 2 tablespoons (30 g) of the Thai green curry paste and the butter beans. Mix for 1 minute over the heat, until everything is coated in the paste.

Turn down the heat slightly, and add the coconut milk and tamari. Bring to a simmer, then simmer for 15 minutes, stirring occasionally, until reduced slightly.

Add the pepper, corn and snow peas to the pan. Simmer for 5 minutes, or until the veg is fork-tender. Remove from the heat and stir through the lime juice. Season to taste with more tamari.

Serve immediately, garnished with cilantro and a wedge of lime for squeezing.

3 Bean Chili Soup

You know how you get soups that are a nourishing, hearty meal in a bowl and leave you feeling all cozy and content? This is one of those! Kidney beans, black beans and black-eyed beans make it lovely and filling, while the spices and tamari (or soy sauce) add a real depth of flavor to the broth. Half of the soup is blended and added back to give it a lovely smooth consistency.

serves 4

1 tbsp (15 ml) olive oil

1 medium yellow (brown) onion, finely diced

Salt and pepper, to taste

4 cloves garlic, minced

1 red bell pepper, finely diced

1 tbsp (7 g) smoked paprika

1 tbsp (7 g) ground cumin

1 tsp crushed chiles

2 tbsp (30 ml) tamari or soy sauce

1 (14-oz [400-g]) can kidney beans with liquid

1 (14-oz [400-g]) can black beans, drained and rinsed

1 (14-oz [400-g]) can black-eyed beans, drained and rinsed

1¼ cups (300 ml) vegan beef or vegetable broth (stock)

2 (14-oz [400-g]) cans chopped tomatoes, blended until smooth

GARNISHES

Plain, unsweetened vegan yogurt

Chile flakes

Chopped fresh cilantro

1 lime, cut into wedges

Add the oil to a large pot over medium heat. Add the onion and a pinch of salt and pepper and sauté for a few minutes, until soft.

Add the garlic and bell pepper and stir for another 2 to 3 minutes, until soft. Add the smoked paprika, cumin, crushed chiles, tamari and ⅓ cup (80 ml) of water to the pot and stir for a minute over the heat.

Add all the beans, including the liquid from the kidney beans, and mix well until they are evenly coated in spices.

Pour in the broth and tomatoes and bring to a simmer. Put a lid on the pot and simmer for about 15 minutes, stirring occasionally. Move half of the soup to a blender and blend until smooth. Return the blended soup to the pot and mix well. Season to taste with salt and pepper.

Serve in bowls topped with a dollop of yogurt and a sprinkle of chile flakes and cilantro. Serve lime wedges on the side to squeeze over before eating.

coconutty curried Beans

This recipe is inspired by the comforting flavors of Korma—think creamy, cozy and fragrant. Hearty chickpeas and butter beans are simmered with aromatics in a creamy coconut milk sauce. It's just as nourishing as it is delicious—earthy carrot is hidden in the sauce while ground almonds add texture and creaminess.

serves 3 to 4

1 tbsp (15 ml) neutral oil

1 medium yellow (brown) onion, finely sliced

Salt, to taste

3 cloves garlic, minced

1 tsp minced ginger

1 tsp ground turmeric

1 tsp ground cumin

1 tsp garam masala

Packed ¾ cup (100 g) grated carrot

⅓ cup (30 g) ground almonds

⅓ cup (25 g) desiccated coconut

1 (14-oz [400-g]) can coconut milk

¾ cup plus 1 tbsp (200 ml) vegetable broth (stock)

1 (14-oz [400-g]) can chickpeas, drained and rinsed

1 (14-oz [400-g]) can cannellini beans, drained and rinsed

Salt and pepper, to taste

GARNISHES

1 tbsp (7 g) toasted almond flakes

1 tbsp (3 g) chopped fresh cilantro

Add the oil to a large pan over medium heat. Add the onion and a pinch of salt and sauté for about 5 minutes, until soft.

Add the garlic, ginger, turmeric, cumin and garam masala. Stir for 1 minute over medium heat until fragrant, then add the carrot.

Add the ground almonds and coconut and mix well before pouring in the coconut milk and broth. Simmer for 5 minutes, stirring occasionally, then use an immersion blender to blend to a smooth, creamy consistency.

Add chickpeas and cannellini beans. Simmer for 15 minutes, until thickened and reduced. Season to taste with salt and pepper.

Serve topped with toasted almonds and cilantro.

maple mustard Beans

This classic sweet and savory flavor combination makes for the most moreish sauce. Both Dijon and whole-grain mustard are used for maximum flavor: The tangy notes of Dijon contrast with the sweetness of the maple syrup while the whole-grain mustard adds that distinctive flavor and texture. I like to serve this with some lemony steamed greens and crusty bread on the side for mopping up that tasty sauce.

serves 2

BEANS

2 tsp (10 ml) neutral oil

1 medium leek, finely sliced

Salt, to taste

1 (14-oz [400-g]) can butter beans, drained and rinsed

¾ cup (140 g) cannellini beans, drained and rinsed

Salt and pepper, to taste

2 tbsp (30 g) whole-grain mustard, plus more to taste

1 tsp Dijon mustard, plus more to taste

1 tbsp (15 ml) maple syrup, plus more to taste

Fresh lemon juice, to taste

Chopped fresh chives, for garnish

CREAMY SAUCE

½ cup (120 ml) vegetable broth (stock)

½ cup (100 g) cannellini beans, drained and rinsed

Salt and pepper, to taste

To make the beans: Add the oil to a large pan over medium-low heat. Add the leek and a pinch of salt and sauté for 5 to 7 minutes, until tender and reduced in volume.

Add the butter and cannellini beans, and season with salt and pepper. Mix well. Add the whole-grain mustard, Dijon mustard and maple syrup to the pan and stir through. Turn off the heat.

To make the sauce: Blend the broth with the cannellini beans until smooth. Season with salt and pepper, then pour it into the pan with the beans and leek.

Place the pan over medium-low heat and simmer for 5 to 10 minutes, until thick and creamy. Squeeze in lemon juice to taste and add more mustard or maple syrup if needed. Serve garnished with chives.

Herby Tahini Beans

Light and fragrant yet creamy and moreish . . . these Herby Tahini Beans have become a go-to midweek dinner. The recipe came about when I had the last of a jar of a tahini to use up and wanted a quick, comforting dinner. If I'm lucky enough to have some left over, they make a flavorful breakfast or brunch the next day heaped on some toasted sourdough.

serves 2

2 tsp (10 ml) olive oil

1 medium yellow (brown) onion, finely sliced

1 green chile, finely diced

4 cloves garlic, minced

¼ tsp ground cumin

¼ tsp ground coriander

1 (14-oz [400-g]) can butter beans, drained and rinsed

1 (14-oz [400-g]) can chickpeas, drained and rinsed, divided

Salt and pepper, to taste

1¾ cups (400 ml) vegetable broth (stock)

¼ cup (60 g) tahini

1 cup (23 g) spinach

Zest of ½ lemon

2 tbsp (6 g) chopped fresh cilantro, plus more to garnish

¼ cup (15 g) chopped fresh parsley, plus more to garnish

2 tbsp (30 ml) fresh lemon juice

Add the oil to a large pan over medium heat. Add the onion and stir over the heat for about 5 minutes, until soft and translucent. Add the chile, garlic, cumin and coriander and stir for another 2 to 3 minutes, until soft and fragrant.

Add the butter beans and half of the chickpeas to the pan and season with a pinch of salt and pepper. Stir for a minute to let the flavors infuse.

Add the remaining half of the chickpeas to a blender or beaker if using an immersion blender. Add the broth and tahini to the chickpeas and blend until smooth.

Pour the creamy chickpea mixture into the pan and stir through. Leave to simmer over medium-low heat for 10 to 15 minutes, until reduced and thickened, stirring occasionally.

Once reduced, stir in the spinach, lemon zest, cilantro and parsley. Once the spinach has wilted, season with salt and pepper to taste and stir in the lemon juice. Serve immediately, topped with a sprinkle of fresh herbs.

edamame, coconut & cilantro soup

Edamame beans work incredibly well in a soup. They add a vibrant green color, a slightly sweet, almost nutty flavor and of course, all-important plant-based protein. The best thing about this recipe is it uses frozen edamame beans and peas, meaning you can whip it up at a moment's notice with just a can of coconut milk and a handful of fresh ingredients.

serves 4

2 tsp (10 ml) coconut oil or neutral oil

1 medium yellow (brown) onion, diced

3 cloves garlic, minced

2 tsp (5 g) minced ginger

1 green chile, diced

2 cups (340 g) frozen edamame

1 cup (150 g) frozen peas

2⅛ cups (500 ml) vegetable broth (stock)

1 (14-oz [400-g]) can coconut milk

Salt and pepper, to taste

1 packed cup (30 g) fresh cilantro

1 tbsp (15 ml) fresh lime juice

OPTIONAL GARNISHES

1–2 tbsp (15–30 ml) coconut milk

Cooked edamame

Chopped cilantro

Lime wedges

Sesame seeds

Add the oil to a large saucepan over medium heat. Add the onion and soften for a few minutes, then add the garlic, ginger and chile. Stir for a couple of minutes, until everything is soft and fragrant. Add the frozen edamame beans and peas. Mix well.

Stir for a minute over the heat to let the beans and peas absorb some of the flavor, then pour in the broth and coconut milk. Bring to a simmer, then simmer for 15 minutes, stirring occasionally.

Use an immersion blender, or pour into a heatproof blender to blend until smooth and creamy. Season to taste with salt and pepper. Add the cilantro and blend again. Once smooth, stir through the lime juice. Serve and add garnishes, if using.

plant-powered mains

Beans are an incredible source of plant-based protein and completely hold their own as the hero ingredient in dishes. Equally, they're an amazing addition to meals alongside other delicious vegetables.

This chapter showcases dishes that are great for dinner, using beans in lots of different ways. Borlotti beans are the star of the Stroganoff Beans with Mushrooms & Garlic Rice (page 47), while butter beans are blended into a gorgeously creamy, umami puree to accompany melt-in-your-mouth roasted hispi cabbage (page 48).

From One-Pan Bean Lasagna (page 62) to Spicy Kidney Bean Burgers with Raita & Mango Chutney (page 67), you'll find everything from tasty spins on classics to fresh ideas and flavors in this chapter of hearty mains.

stroganoff Beans with mushrooms & Garlic Rice

Rich and creamy with a subtle sharpness, this is a hearty, warming dish that I make again and again. The garlic rice is worth the extra couple of minutes of prep—it really takes this dish to a whole new level of comfort food.

serves 2

GARLIC RICE

1 tbsp (15 ml) olive oil

4 cloves garlic, minced

⅔ cup (125 g) long-grain rice, rinsed

¼ tsp salt

2 tbsp (8 g) chopped fresh parsley, plus more to garnish

STROGANOFF BEANS WITH MUSHROOMS

1 tbsp (15 ml) olive oil

1 medium white onion, finely sliced

Salt, to taste

3 cloves garlic, minced

3 cups (300 g) chestnut mushrooms, roughly chopped

1 (14-oz [400-g]) can borlotti beans, drained and rinsed

Black pepper, to taste

1 tsp marmite

1 tsp tomato paste

1 tsp Dijon mustard

¾ cup plus 1 tbsp (200 ml) vegetable broth (stock)

½ cup (120 g) plain, unsweetened vegan yogurt

1–2 tsp (5–10 ml) fresh lemon juice

To make the garlic rice: Add the oil to a saucepan over low heat. Add the garlic and stir for 1 to 2 minutes, until fragrant and golden. Add the rinsed rice and stir for a minute until slightly translucent.

Cover the rice with 1⅓ cups (315 ml) of water and add the salt. Bring to a simmer and allow the rice to absorb the water. Once almost all the water has been absorbed, turn the heat off and cover it with a lid. Leave it to sit for about 10 minutes, then fluff with a fork.

While the rice is cooking, start the stroganoff: Add the oil to a large pan along with the onion and a pinch of salt. Soften for about 5 minutes, until translucent. Add the garlic and soften for 1 to 2 minutes.

Add the mushrooms and sauté for 5 minutes, or until the mushrooms reduce slightly and start to color. Add the beans and season well with salt and pepper. Stir to combine.

Add the marmite, tomato paste and mustard. Mix well. Stir in the broth and bring to a simmer. Reduce for 5 to 10 minutes. Stir in the yogurt, then season to taste with salt and pepper. Stir through the lemon juice just before serving.

Stir the parsley through the fluffed rice. Serve the stroganoff alongside the garlic rice, topped with more parsley.

Roasted Hispi Cabbage, Salsa Verde & Tahini Bean Puree

Roasting hispi cabbage gives it the most delicious, sweet, nutty and caramelized flavor. The tender cabbage wedges sit on top of a seriously creamy bean puree and a tangy salsa verde cuts through everything. It's then topped with golden chile breadcrumbs for crunch.

Serves 2

ROASTED CABBAGE

1 large hispi (sweetheart) cabbage, quartered

1 tbsp (15 ml) olive oil

½ tsp salt

TAHINI BEAN PUREE

1 (14-oz [400-g]) can butter beans, drained and rinsed

2 tbsp (30 g) tahini

½ tsp salt

Black pepper, to taste

1 clove garlic

Zest of 1 lemon

2 tbsp (30 ml) fresh lemon juice, plus more to taste

SALSA VERDE

3 tbsp (12 g) chopped fresh parsley

1 tbsp (5 g) chopped fresh mint

1 tbsp (9 g) capers, finely chopped

3 tbsp (45 ml) extra virgin olive oil

1 tbsp (15 ml) white wine vinegar

¼ tsp salt

Preheat the oven to 425°F (220°C or gas mark 7).

To make the cabbage: Remove any loose outer leaves from the cabbage quarters, drizzle with oil and season with the salt. Lay on a baking tray with one cut side facing up. Roast for 15 minutes, then flip the cabbage so the other cut side is on the tray. Roast for 10 to 15 minutes, until the cabbage is soft and the edges are golden.

While the cabbage is roasting, make the tahini bean puree: Add the beans, tahini, salt, pepper, garlic, lemon zest, lemon juice and 2 tablespoons (30 ml) of water to a blender or food processor. Blend until smooth and creamy and season to taste with salt, pepper and/or lemon juice. Add a splash more water if needed.

To make the salsa verde: Mix the herbs, capers, oil, vinegar and salt.

(continued)

Roasted Hispi Cabbage, Salsa Verde & Tahini Bean Puree (continued)

CHILE BREADCRUMBS

½ cup (30 g) breadcrumbs

1 tsp (5 ml) extra virgin olive oil

1 tsp Aleppo (pul biber) pepper or ½ tsp chile flakes

¼ tsp salt

To make the breadcrumbs: Add the breadcrumbs to a small pan with the oil, Aleppo pepper and salt. Toast over medium-low heat for a few minutes, until crispy and golden, stirring to make sure they don't burn.

Spread the puree in the center of two plates and place two quarters of roasted cabbage on each. Top with the salsa verde and a sprinkle of breadcrumbs.

squash & Bean Tagine With Herby couscous

There's something satisfying about prepping a cozy, hearty dish and then popping it into the oven to finish off cooking. While your kitchen fills with tempting aromas, you have some time to potter about and get tidied up, knowing you'll be tucking into something tasty very soon. Even if you don't make this wholesome meal in a traditional tagine dish, the concept still stands: slow cooking that builds layers of flavor with fragrant spices, garlic and veg . . . with the addition of protein-packed beans, of course!

serves 2

SQUASH & BEAN TAGINE

1 tbsp (15 ml) olive oil

1 medium yellow (brown) onion, finely sliced

3 cloves garlic, minced

1 tsp ground coriander

1 tsp ground cumin

½ tsp ground cinnamon

⅔ cup (300 g) butternut squash, cut into chunks

1 tbsp (15 g) tomato paste

¼ cup (45 g) dried apricots

1 (14-oz [400-g]) can butter beans, drained and rinsed

1 (14-oz [400-g]) can chopped tomatoes, with liquid

1 cup (240 ml) vegetable broth (stock)

Salt and pepper, to taste

To make the tagine: Preheat the oven to 400°F (200°C or gas mark 6).

Add the oil to a large ovenproof tagine or casserole pot with a lid over medium heat. Add the onion and soften for about 5 minutes, until translucent.

Add the garlic to the pan and soften it for 1 to 2 minutes, before adding the coriander, cumin, cinnamon and butternut squash. Stir over the heat for 5 minutes and allow to soften.

Add the tomato paste, dried apricots and beans and mix well, letting the beans absorb the flavor. Add the tomatoes and broth and mix very well. Put the pan into the oven to bake for 45 minutes, or until the squash is soft and cooked through.

(continued)

squash & Bean Tagine with Herby couscous (continued)

HERBY COUSCOUS

⅔ cup (120 g) couscous

¾ cup (180 ml) warm vegetable broth (stock)

1 tbsp (3 g) chopped fresh cilantro

1 tbsp (4 g) chopped fresh parsley

Zest of 1 lemon

GARNISHES

Chopped fresh parsley

Toasted almond flakes

Meanwhile, prepare the couscous: Add the couscous to a large bowl and pour in the warm broth. Cover and leave for 5 minutes to soak up the broth. Use a fork to fluff up the couscous, then stir the herbs and lemon zest through.

Carefully remove the pot from the oven and season to taste with salt and pepper. Serve the tagine in bowls along with the couscous. Top with parsley and toasted almond flakes.

Garlicky White Beans with Harissa Roasted Tomatoes

It doesn't get much more comforting than rich, garlicky white beans, and the harissa roasted tomatoes add such a pop of flavor to this dish. They turn sweet, sticky and jammy in the oven and contrast perfectly with the creamy sauce of the beans.

serves 2

HARISSA ROASTED TOMATOES

1⅔ cups (250 g) cherry tomatoes

¼ tsp salt

1 tbsp (15 g) harissa

2 tsp (10 ml) olive oil

GARLICKY WHITE BEANS

½ medium yellow (brown) onion, finely sliced

2 tsp (10 ml) olive oil

¼ tsp salt

4 cloves garlic

1 (14-oz [400-g]) can cannellini beans, plus ¼ cup (60 ml) liquid from can

1 cup (240 ml) vegetable broth (stock)

⅔ cup (150 ml) unsweetened soymilk

1 tbsp (3 g) nutritional yeast

Chopped fresh parsley, for garnish

Chile flakes, for garnish

To make the tomatoes: Preheat the oven to 425°F (220°C or gas mark 7).

Add the tomatoes to an ovenproof dish with the salt, harissa and oil. Stir to coat the tomatoes. Roast them for 20 to 25 minutes, until blistered and jammy. Use the back of a spoon to smoosh them down to a thick puree and set aside.

While the tomatoes are roasting, prepare the garlicky beans: Add the onion and oil to a medium pan over medium heat. Fry the onion with the salt for about 5 minutes, until translucent, then add the garlic. Stir for 1 minute, then add 2 tablespoons (30 ml) of water to the pan. Stir for 1 to 2 minutes, until the liquid has reduced, then add the beans with the reserved liquid.

Mix well before adding the broth. Turn up the heat slightly and simmer for about 10 minutes to reduce the liquid, stirring occasionally. Once reduced, turn the heat down to medium-low and stir in the soymilk and nutritional yeast.

Remove one-quarter of the contents of the pan and add it to a blender, or use an immersion blender, to blend until smooth. Add the mixture back to the pan, and stir to combine with the sauce in the pan.

Continue to simmer until thick and creamy. Serve the beans in bowls with jammy tomatoes on top, garnished with chopped parsley and chile flakes.

miso mac & beans with chile crumb

Mac and cheese, meet mac and beans. My spin on the comfort food classic is loaded with lots of umami miso to give the "cheesy" sauce extra tang. That's where the beans come in—cannellini beans are blended to give the sauce a super creamy consistency. The flavor is taken to the next level with a crunchy cashew crumb topping.

serves 2

MISO MAC

1½ cups (190 g) macaroni

1 (14-oz [400-g]) can cannellini beans, drained and rinsed

⅓ cup plus 1½ tbsp (100 ml) unsweetened soymilk

⅓ cup (25 g) nutritional yeast

1 tsp garlic granules

2 tsp (10 g) Dijon mustard

1½ tbsp (25 g) miso

2 tsp (10 ml) apple cider vinegar

Salt and pepper, to taste

CHILE CRUMB

¼ cup (45 g) cashews

2 tbsp (6 g) nutritional yeast

1 tsp chile flakes

¼ tsp garlic granules

¼ tsp salt

To make the mac: Bring a large pot of salted water to boil before adding the macaroni. Cook according to the package instructions until al dente, then drain.

While the pasta is boiling, make the sauce: Add the cannellini beans, soymilk, nutritional yeast, garlic granules, mustard, miso and vinegar to a blender. Blend until smooth.

To make the crumb: Add the cashews, nutritional yeast, chile flakes, garlic granules and salt to a small blender cup or beaker if using an immersion blender. Blend to a crumb-like consistency.

Return the drained pasta to the pan and pour in the sauce. Stir over medium-low heat until piping hot. Season to taste with salt and pepper.

Serve the macaroni topped with the "cheesy" chile crumb.

mushroom & Butter Bean Filo pie

If you've never tried using filo pastry to top a pie, you're missing out! Butter beans, mushrooms and artichokes are cooked in the creamiest sauce, flavored with garlic and thyme. The marinated artichokes create a slightly "meaty" texture and a subtly sharp flavor that adds a richness to the sauce, almost like white wine. I love pairing this with the Creamy Butter Bean & Mustard Mash on page 131.

serves 3 to 4

1 tbsp (15 ml) oil from the jar of artichokes

2 large French Echalion (banana) shallots, finely sliced

1 cup (225 g) marinated artichoke hearts, finely chopped

5 cloves garlic, minced

8 sprigs of thyme, leaves stripped, divided

5 cups (500 g) mushrooms, roughly chopped

1 (14-oz [400-g]) can butter beans, drained and rinsed

Salt and pepper, to taste

1 tbsp (8 g) all-purpose (plain) flour

1¾ cups (400 ml) mushroom or vegetable broth (stock)

⅓ cup (85 g) plain, unsweetened vegan yogurt

4–5 sheets of filo pastry

1 tbsp (15 ml) olive oil, for brushing

Preheat the oven to 350°F (180°C or gas mark 4).

On the stovetop, heat the 1 tablespoon (15 ml) of oil from the artichokes in a round ovenproof pan or dish. Add the shallots and fry them over medium heat for about 5 minutes, or until soft. Add the artichokes, garlic and 6 sprigs of thyme and fry for another couple of minutes.

Add the mushrooms to the pan and soften for about 10 minutes, until they reduce considerably in size. Don't stir too much to allow them to take on some color. Add the butter beans, season with salt and pepper and mix well.

Add the flour and stir through everything in the pan. Pour the broth in and deglaze any flavor from the bottom of the pan.

Bring the pan to a simmer and keep stirring as the mixture thickens. Add the yogurt and mix well to combine it into the sauce.

Tear the filo pastry into narrow strips. Scrunch and fold each strip on top of the mushroom and bean filling. Once the whole pan is covered, use a fork to tuck any loose edges of pastry down into the filling.

Brush the pastry lightly with oil and sprinkle the remaining thyme leaves over it. Bake for about 20 minutes, or until the pastry is golden and crispy. Serve immediately.

Pesto Beans with "Cheesy" Potato Wedges

Forget pesto pasta, pesto beans are where it's at. They're packed with protein, fiber, iron and magnesium without compromising on flavor. Team them with some crispy "cheesy" garlic wedges and we're talking next level comfort food that's as good for the body as it is for the soul.

Serves 2

"CHEESY" GARLIC WEDGES

2 medium potatoes

1 tbsp (3 g) nutritional yeast

1 tsp garlic granules

½ tsp salt

1 tbsp (15 ml) olive oil

SPINACH PESTO

1 cup (30 g) fresh basil

Packed ¾ cup (21 g) spinach

¼ cup (20 g) nutritional yeast

2 cloves garlic

¼ tsp salt

BEANS

2 tsp (10 ml) olive oil

½ cup (75 g) jarred sun-dried tomatoes, finely chopped

2 medium shallots, finely sliced

1 (14-oz [400-g]) can cannellini beans, drained and rinsed

Salt and pepper, to taste

1 cup (240 ml) vegetable broth (stock)

1 tbsp (15 ml) fresh lemon juice

GARNISHES

1 tbsp (8 g) toasted pine nuts

Fresh basil leaves

TO SERVE

2 cups (50 g) arugula

To make the wedges: Preheat the oven to 400°F (200°C or gas mark 6) or air fryer to 350°F (180°C).

Slice the potatoes into wedges and add them to a large bowl along with the nutritional yeast, garlic granules, salt and oil. Bake for 20 to 25 minutes or air fry for 15 to 20 minutes, or until the wedges are crispy and golden outside and fluffy inside.

While the wedges are cooking, start making the pesto and beans. For the pesto, add the basil, spinach, nutritional yeast, garlic and salt to a blender, or a beaker if using an immersion blender, and blend until smooth. Set aside.

To make the beans, add the oil, sun-dried tomatoes and shallots to a medium-sized pan and soften for about 5 minutes over medium heat. Add the cannellini beans and season with salt and pepper.

Pour in the pesto and broth and simmer for 5 to 10 minutes, or until reduced and thickened. Season to taste with salt and pepper and stir through the lemon juice just before serving.

Serve the pesto beans topped with a sprinkle of toasted pine nuts and fresh basil, alongside the potato wedges and a large handful of arugula (rocket).

one-Pan Bean Lasagna

Lasagna can sometimes be a bit of an effort, but this one keeps things super simple. Borlotti beans are cooked with a soffritto of onion, carrot and celery, chopped tomatoes and broth to pack in maximum flavor. There's no need to make a roux or spend time thickening sauces here. Simply blend up the creamy sauce and layer with the beans and lasagna sheets. Perfecto!

serves 4

LASAGNA

2 tsp (10 ml) olive oil

½ medium carrot, finely diced

1 rib celery, finely diced

½ medium yellow (brown) onion, finely diced

3 cloves garlic, minced

2 (14-oz [400-g]) cans borlotti beans, divided

Salt and pepper, to taste

2 (14-oz [400-g]) cans chopped tomatoes

2 vegan beef or vegetable stock/bouillon cubes

5 lasagna sheets

CREAMY SAUCE

1 (14-oz [400-g]) can cannellini beans, drained and rinsed

3 tbsp (12 g) nutritional yeast, divided

¾ cup plus 1 tbsp (200 ml) unsweetened soymilk

1 tsp garlic granules

¼ tsp salt

1 tbsp (15 ml) fresh lemon juice

TO SERVE

2 cups (40 g) arugula

1 tsp extra virgin olive oil

1 tsp balsamic vinegar

To make the lasagna: Preheat the oven to 350°F (180°C or gas mark 4).

Add the oil to an ovenproof dish along with the carrot, celery and onion. Sauté for at least 10 minutes, or until soft—don't rush, as this is where all the flavor comes from. Add the garlic and soften for 1 to 2 minutes.

Add one can of the beans to the pan. Use the back of a spoon to press down and break them up as much as possible—you might have to push down quite hard. Once most of the beans are broken down, add the second can of beans and season really well with salt and pepper.

Pour in the tomatoes. Mix the stock cubes with ¾ cup plus 1 tbsp (200 ml) of boiling water, add to the pan and mix well. Simmer on low for 5 minutes.

Meanwhile make the creamy sauce: Add the beans, 2 tablespoons (6 g) of the nutritional yeast, soymilk, garlic granules, salt and lemon juice to a blender or food processor and blend until smooth.

Break the lasagna sheets in half. Submerge them in the tomato sauce, in a flat layer about ½ inch (1 cm) below the surface. Pour the creamy sauce over the beans and lasagna sheets until the full surface is covered. Top with the remaining 1 tablespoon (3 g) of nutritional yeast. Bake for 30 to 40 minutes, or until the pasta sheets are al dente.

Toss the arugula with the oil and vinegar. Serve the dressed arugula alongside the lasagna.

herby green chermoula Beans

This recipe is inspired by a green shakshuka that I ordered in a restaurant a couple of years back and haven't stopped thinking about since. The fresh, herby flavors of the fragrant sauce are soaked up by earthy butter beans and chickpeas. It's all finished off with a drizzle of lemon garlic yogurt and some more of the vibrant, moreish sauce.

serves 2

BEANS

2 tsp (10 ml) olive oil

1 medium onion, finely sliced

¼ tsp salt, plus more to taste

2 cloves garlic, minced

1 medium leek, finely sliced

1 medium green bell pepper, sliced

1 tsp ground cumin

1 (14-oz [400-g]) can butter beans, drained and rinsed

1 (14-oz [400-g]) can chickpeas, drained and rinsed

2 cups (480 ml) vegetable broth (stock), divided

HERBY CHERMOULA

2 tsp (4 g) cumin seeds

2 tsp (4 g) coriander seeds

2 cups (60 g) fresh cilantro

2 cups (60 g) chopped fresh parsley

2 cloves garlic

2 tsp (10 ml) fresh lemon juice

Zest of 1 lemon

1 tsp Aleppo (pul biber) chile

2 tbsp (30 ml) olive oil

½ tsp salt

To make the beans: Heat the oil in a large pan. Add the onion and the salt. Fry for about 5 minutes over medium heat, until soft and lightly golden. Add the garlic and leek, then soften for 5 minutes. Add the bell pepper and cumin, and stir for 2 minutes.

Add the butter beans and chickpeas to the pan and season with a pinch of salt. Stir over the heat for a minute to absorb the flavors. Add 1 cup (240 ml) of the broth and simmer over low heat for 15 minutes or so, stirring now and again.

As the beans simmer, make the herby chermoula: In a dry pan, toast the cumin and coriander seeds for 1 to 2 minutes, until golden and fragrant. Add the toasted spices to a food processor and pulse a few times to a fine powder. Add the cilantro, parsley, garlic, lemon juice and zest, chile, oil, salt and 1 tablespoon (15 ml) of water to the food processor. Blend until smooth. You may need to scrape down the sides using a spatula in between blends.

Add three-quarters of the chermoula to the pan with the beans, along with the remaining 1 cup (240 ml) of broth. Leave to simmer for 10 minutes, until the liquid reduces, stirring now and again.

(continued)

Herby Green Chermoula Beans
(continued)

LEMON GARLIC YOGURT

¼ cup (60 g) plain, unsweetened vegan yogurt

1 tbsp (15 ml) fresh lemon juice

1 clove garlic, minced

¼ tsp salt

Chile flakes, for garnish

Meanwhile, make the lemon garlic yogurt: Add the yogurt, lemon juice, garlic and salt to a small bowl. Mix well.

Serve the beans and chickpeas topped with some of the yogurt and the remaining chermoula drizzled over. Finish with a sprinkle of chile flakes.

spicy Kidney Bean Burgers with Raita & mango chutney

Bean burgers have a bit of a reputation for being the token veggie option, and I wanted to change that. These burgers are made with a base of protein-packed kidney beans and paired with cooling raita-style yogurt, sweet mango chutney and pink pickled onions to liven things up. These flavor-packed burgers will be everyone's top choice, omnivores and vegans alike.

serves 2

PINK PICKLED ONIONS

½ medium red onion, thinly sliced

2 tbsp (15 ml) fresh lime juice

2 tbsp (15 ml) apple cider vinegar

½ tsp ground cumin

BEAN BURGERS

1 (14-oz [400-g]) can kidney beans, drained and rinsed

⅓ cup (30 g) breadcrumbs

Packed ⅓ cup (15 g) fresh cilantro

½ tsp garlic granules

½ tsp onion granules

1 tsp ground cumin

½ tsp chili powder

½ tsp garam masala

1 tbsp (15 ml) tamari or light soy sauce

1 tsp (5 ml) olive oil

To make the pickled onions: Add the onion to a small bowl and cover with the lime juice, vinegar and cumin. Leave to one side to pickle while you make the burgers.

To make the burgers: Preheat the oven to 400°F (200°C or gas mark 6) or air fryer to 350°F (180°C). If using the oven, line a baking tray with parchment paper.

Add the beans, breadcrumbs, cilantro, garlic granules, onion granules, cumin, chili powder, garam masala, tamari and oil to a food processor. Pulse until the mixture is mostly smooth with a little bit of texture, scraping down the bowl using a spatula if needed.

Shape the mixture into two patties and brush both sides with oil. Either place onto the lined tray or into the basket of your air fryer.

Bake in the oven for about 20 minutes or air fry for about 15 minutes, turning halfway through, until firm.

(continued)

Spicy Kidney Bean Burgers with Raita & Mango Chutney (continued)

RAITA-STYLE YOGURT

⅓ cup (60 g) grated cucumber

¼ cup (60 g) plain, unsweetened vegan yogurt

1 tbsp (2 g) chopped fresh mint

¼ tsp salt

TO SERVE

2 vegan burger buns

Small handful spinach leaves

2 tbsp (35 g) mango chutney

While the burgers are cooking, make the raita-style yogurt: Squeeze out any excess liquid from the cucumber. Add it to a small bowl with the yogurt, mint and salt. Mix well.

Lightly toast the burger buns. Spread the bottom of each with the yogurt and add a handful of spinach. Add the bean burger and top with the mango chutney and pickled onions. Place the bun tops on and serve.

orange Gochujang Noodles with Tofu & Edamame

I don't know about you, but noodles are one of those things that I'm always in the mood for. This recipe really delivers on plant-based protein with both crispy tofu and edamame beans. It's super versatile in that you can bulk it up with any veg, whatever you have to hand. I love adding some shredded pak choi in with the noodles, but shiitake mushrooms, peppers and onion are also great.

serves 2

CRISPY TOFU

7 oz (200 g) extra firm tofu, drained and cut into small cubes

Salt and pepper, to taste

1 tbsp (10 g) cornstarch

1 tbsp (15 ml) sesame oil

ORANGE GOCHUJANG NOODLES

2 portions whole wheat noodles

1 cup (150 g) frozen edamame

2 tsp (8 g) gochujang

1 tbsp (15 ml) agave

1 tsp minced garlic

2 tbsp (30 ml) tamari or light soy sauce

2 tsp (10 ml) rice vinegar

¾ cup (175 ml) fresh orange juice

2 tsp (6 g) cornstarch

GARNISHES

1 tsp sesame seeds

1 spring onion, finely sliced

To make the tofu: Toss the tofu in a medium-sized bowl with the salt, pepper and cornstarch. Add the oil to a medium-sized pan over medium heat. Add the tofu and fry for around 5 minutes, until golden and crispy on all sides. Remove the tofu from the pan and put it to one side.

To make the noodles: Cook the noodles according to package instructions. Cook the edamame beans in a medium-sized pan of boiling water for 5 minutes. Rinse with cold water and drain.

Add the gochujang, agave, garlic, tamari, vinegar and orange juice to a medium-sized bowl and whisk to combine. Pour the sauce into the pan and bring to a gentle simmer.

In a small bowl or mug, mix the cornstarch with 2 teaspoons (10 ml) of water. Mix with a fork to combine.

Making sure the sauce is simmering in the pan, pour in the cornstarch slurry and whisk continuously until the sauce thickens. Add the noodles, edamame and tofu, and mix to coat in the sauce.

Once everything is piping hot, serve topped with sesame seeds and spring onion.

Mediterranean Tray Bake with Quick Pesto

There's nothing better than a one-pan dinner, and this tray bake is no exception. I like to think of the butter beans as a high-protein, nutrient-packed version of gnocchi, soaking up all the flavor of the tomato sauce and roasted veg. It's all topped off with a vibrant green pesto and served with leafy arugula.

serves 2

MEDITERRANEAN TRAY BAKE

1½ cups (200 g) cherry tomatoes

1 medium red onion, chopped into ½-inch (1-cm) pieces

1 medium zucchini, sliced into half moons

1 red pepper, chopped into ½-inch (1-cm) pieces

½ tsp salt, plus more to taste

1 tsp dried oregano

½ tsp garlic granules

1 tbsp (15 ml) olive oil

1 (14-oz [400-g]) can butter beans, drained and rinsed

Black pepper, to taste

1¾ cups (400 ml) passata or chopped tomatoes, with liquid

1 tsp smoked paprika

1 vegetable stock/bouillon cube

⅓ cup (60 g) black olives, sliced

QUICK PESTO

1 cup (30 g) fresh basil

1 tsp fresh lemon juice

1 tbsp (15 ml) extra virgin olive oil

1 tbsp (3 g) nutritional yeast

¼ tsp salt

2 cups (40 g) arugula, to serve

To make the tray bake: Preheat the oven to 400°F (200°C or gas mark 6).

Add the tomatoes, onion, zucchini and pepper to a large, deep oven tray or dish. Season with the salt. Sprinkle with oregano and garlic granules, and drizzle with the oil. Stir the vegetables to coat. Roast the vegetables in the oven for 25 minutes.

While the veg is roasting, season the beans with salt and pepper.

In a medium bowl, mix the passata with the smoked paprika and crumble in the stock cube.

Add the butter beans and olives to the roasted vegetables and cover with the tomato mix. Roast for 25 minutes.

Meanwhile, make the quick pesto: Add the basil, lemon juice, oil, nutritional yeast and salt to a small blender cup, or beaker if using an immersion blender. Blend until smooth.

Serve the roasted veg and beans topped with the pesto with the arugula on the side.

Turmeric Beans with Cumin Roasted Cauliflower

Roasting veg with some kind of herb or spice is one of my favorite ways to pack flavor into a dish. I make this cumin-roasted cauliflower a lot (it's always my mum's top request if I'm cooking for her!), and I knew I wanted it to have a place in this book. I've teamed it with some warming turmeric beans. Turmeric not only gives the beans a beautiful, golden color, it also adds a lovely earthy flavor.

serves 2

CUMIN ROASTED CAULIFLOWER

2½ cups (275 g) cauliflower, chopped into florets

¼ tsp salt

1 tbsp (15 ml) olive oil

1 tsp cumin seeds

TURMERIC BEANS

1 tbsp (15 ml) neutral oil

1 medium yellow (brown) onion, finely sliced

Salt and pepper, to taste

3 cloves garlic, minced

1 tsp minced ginger

1 tsp ground turmeric

½ tsp chile flakes

1 (14-oz [400-g]) can butter beans, drained and rinsed

1 (14-oz [400-g]) can chickpeas, drained and rinsed

¾ cup (180 ml) coconut milk

1 vegetable stock/bouillon cube

1 tsp fresh lemon juice, plus more to taste

GARNISHES

1 green chile, sliced

Fresh cilantro

To make the cauliflower: Preheat the oven to 400°F (200°C or gas mark 6) or air fryer to 350°F (180°C).

Spread the cauliflower over a baking tray. Season with the salt and drizzle with the oil. Sprinkle with cumin seeds and stir on the tray to coat the cauliflower.

Roast for 20 to 25 minutes or air fry for 15 to 20 minutes, until the cauliflower is soft and golden on the edges.

While the cauliflower is roasting, start preparing the beans: Add the oil and onion to a large pan with a pinch of salt and pepper. Soften over medium heat for about 5 minutes before adding the garlic, ginger, turmeric and chile flakes. Soften everything for a couple of minutes, until fragrant.

Add the butter beans and chickpeas, and season well with salt and pepper. Stir for a minute over the heat to let the beans and chickpeas absorb the flavors from the pan.

Add the coconut milk and crumble in the stock cube. Mix well and bring to a gentle simmer. Let the liquid simmer and reduce for about 10 minutes. Just before serving, squeeze in the lemon juice, adding more to taste if needed.

Serve the beans in bowls topped with the roasted cauliflower and green chile and cilantro for garnish.

Sticky Harissa Butter Beans with Pomegranate & Pistachio Quinoa

A little bit sweet and a little bit spicy, this dish is a sure-fire stand out. The beans and eggplant are marinated in harissa, maple syrup and garlic, then roasted until sticky. They're heaped onto herby quinoa, full of juicy pomegranate jewels, and then finished with a drizzle of creamy yogurt dressing.

serves 2

STICKY HARISSA BUTTER BEANS & EGGPLANT

1 (14-oz [400-g]) can butter beans, drained and rinsed

¼ tsp salt

3 cups (260 g) eggplant, chopped into chunks

3 tbsp (45 g) harissa

1½ tbsp (22 g) maple syrup

1 clove garlic, minced

1 tbsp (15 ml) olive oil

QUINOA

½ cup (80 g) quinoa

¼ tsp salt

1½ tbsp (22 ml) fresh lemon juice

½ cup (80 g) pomegranate seeds

2 tbsp (8 g) chopped fresh parsley

1 tbsp (2 g) chopped fresh mint

YOGURT DRESSING

2 tbsp (30 g) plain, unsweetened vegan yogurt

1 tsp harissa

1 tbsp (15 ml) fresh lemon juice

½ tsp maple syrup

¼ tsp salt

GARNISH

2 tbsp (12 g) chopped pistachios

Preheat the oven to 400°F (200°C or gas mark 6). Line a baking tray with parchment paper.

To make the beans and eggplant: Add the butter beans to a large bowl and season with the salt. Add the eggplant, harissa, maple syrup, garlic and oil.

Spread the marinated beans and eggplant over the tray. Roast for 15 minutes. Remove the tray from the oven, stir the beans and eggplant, then return the tray to the oven to roast for 15 minutes, or until the eggplant is soft.

While the eggplant and beans are roasting, make the quinoa: Add the quinoa to a medium-sized pan with a lid. Cover with 1½ cups (350 ml) of water and the salt and bring to a simmer. Simmer for 10 minutes, or until almost all the liquid has reduced. Remove the pan from the heat and cover with the lid. Leave to stand for at least 5 minutes.

Fluff up the quinoa with a fork and add to a large bowl. Add the lemon juice, pomegranate seeds, parsley and mint.

To make the dressing: Combine the yogurt, harissa, lemon juice, syrup and salt in a small bowl.

Serve the quinoa topped with the roasted eggplant and butter beans. Drizzle with the dressing and top with chopped pistachios.

super-green spaghetti

Spaghetti has never looked more vibrant! The super-green sauce is so quick and easy to make: Cannellini beans are blended with leafy spinach, basil, nutritional yeast and lemon. Stir it through the spaghetti, and you're done!

serves 2

6.35 oz (180 g) dried spaghetti

SUPER-GREEN SAUCE

¾ cup (120 g) canned cannellini beans, drained and rinsed

1 clove garlic

1 cup (35 g) spinach

¾ cup (30 g) fresh basil

2 tbsp (6 g) nutritional yeast

1 tbsp (30 ml) fresh lemon juice

¼ tsp salt, plus more to taste

Black pepper, to taste

TO SERVE

1 tbsp (8 g) toasted pine nuts or sunflower seeds

Fresh basil leaves

Extra virgin olive oil

Cook the spaghetti in a large pot of boiling, salted water according to package instructions until al dente.

While the pasta is cooking, make the sauce: Add the cannellini beans, garlic, spinach, basil, nutritional yeast, lemon juice and salt to a food processor or blender and blend until smooth. Season to taste with more salt if needed.

Drain the pasta and return it to the pot. Pour in the sauce and stir over low heat until warmed through. Season to taste with salt and pepper.

Serve the pasta in bowls topped with toasted pine nuts, fresh basil and a drizzle of oil.

Fresh, Flavorsome Salads & Bowls

When you think of meals with beans, I can almost guarantee your mind goes to cozy, hearty dishes that are synonymous with colder days. Hopefully by the time you finish this chapter, you'll be convinced that they work just as well in light, fresh salads and bowls.

Beans make incredible bases for salads and bowls: they are nutrient dense, and they also take on flavor amazingly well. And, of course, a good salad is nothing without a dressing, so I spent a lot of time perfecting each one—making sure the flavors contrast, complement or enhance the ingredients in each dish. Salads aren't just for summer, either! While a couple of the recipes, such as the White Bean Panzanella Salad (page 83), lend themselves well to the seasonal produce of the summer months, most of them are well suited to any time of year. No matter the weather, you can tuck into a tasty dish packed with flavor—and plenty fiber and protein, too.

All the salads and bowls in this chapter are full of vibrant textures, tastes and colors. The Antipasti Bean Salad (page 92) uses mostly pantry ingredients—it's perfect for making when the fridge is almost empty but you still fancy something fresh and flavorsome. I've created some twists on classics, such as the Caesar-Style Crispy Butter Bean Salad (page 87) and the Charred Lettuce Wedges with Ranch-Style Dressing & Beany "Bacon" Bits (page 91), using beans as an alternative for other key ingredients and an important vehicle for flavor. It would be impossible to pick a favorite, but the Edamame "Sushi" Salad with Sesame Soy Dressing (page 88) is definitely up there. It brings together all the familiar ingredients of sushi, even down to the pickled ginger and wasabi.

White Bean Panzanella Salad

Is there anything better than the sweet smell of perfectly ripe tomatoes? It instantly takes me back to summer days spent in my grandad's greenhouse . . . there's nothing better! This is one to make in the summer when tomatoes are at their best, days are long and you're craving something light and fresh. Crispy butter beans are used instead of bread to soak up all the flavor from the tomatoes while introducing a key textural contrast. Heaven!

serves 2 as a main or 4 as a side

CRISPY BUTTER BEANS

1 (14-oz [400-g]) can butter beans, drained, rinsed and patted dry

1 tbsp (15 ml) olive oil

¼ tsp salt

SALAD

2½ cups (500 g) heritage tomatoes, sliced

Salt and pepper, to taste

¼ cup (60 ml) extra virgin olive oil

2½ tbsp (38 ml) red wine vinegar

2 cloves garlic, minced

To make the beans: Preheat the oven to 425°F (220°C or gas mark 7). Line a baking tray with parchment paper.

Spread with beans over the tray. Drizzle with oil and sprinkle with the salt. Stir the beans on the tray, then roast them for 12 to 15 minutes, until golden and crispy. Remove the tray from the oven and leave to cool.

Meanwhile, make the salad: Add all the tomatoes to a large mixing bowl and season well with salt and pepper. Gently toss to make sure each slice is seasoned.

After a few minutes, drain any juice from the tomatoes into a smaller bowl and stir in the oil, vinegar and garlic.

Add the beans to the bowl with the tomatoes and pour in the dressing. Gently toss everything together.

Serve on a large platter or serving plate.

charred corn, Bean & Tomato salad with zingy cilantro Dressing

This salad comes together in no time at all. Once everything is chopped, it's just a matter of tossing it all together in a bowl and adding the vibrant dressing. I honestly can't stress enough how tasty this one is: the bright, bold colors are mirrored in the flavor. There's sweetness, sharpness, earthiness, crunch and heat, and I promise you'll keep coming back for more.

serves 3 to 4

PINK PICKLED ONIONS
½ red onion, finely sliced
3 tbsp (45 ml) apple cider vinegar

CHARRED CORN
1 tsp neutral oil
1 cup (155 g) drained, canned sweet corn
¼ tsp salt

SALAD
1 (14-oz [400-g]) can black beans, drained and rinsed
1 (14-oz [400-g]) can kidney beans, drained and rinsed
Salt and pepper, to taste
1 mango, diced
1 cup (145 g) cherry tomatoes, quartered
2 spring onions, finely sliced

ZINGY CILANTRO DRESSING
Packed ½ cup (30 g) fresh cilantro
3 tbsp (45 ml) vinegar from pickled onions
1 tbsp (12 g) jarred, sliced jalapeños
1 tsp agave

To make the pickled onions: In a small bowl, cover the onion with the vinegar. Leave to one side to pickle for at least 30 minutes.

To make the corn: Add the oil to a nonstick pan and cook the corn with the salt over medium heat for 5 to 7 minutes, until charred on the edges. Stir to make sure it doesn't stick.

To make the salad: Add the black beans and kidney beans to a large mixing bowl. Season well with salt and pepper. Add the mango, tomatoes and spring onions along with the charred corn and pickled onions.

To make the dressing: Add the cilantro, vinegar, sliced jalapeños and agave to a small blender, or beaker if using an immersion blender. Blend until smooth.

Pour the dressing into the large bowl and toss. Season to taste and serve.

caesar-style crispy Butter Bean salad

Classic Caesar salad is made with chicken, but I've switched it up in this adaption and used roasted herby butter beans as the protein source. They're tossed in a mix of herbs, olive oil and lemon for maximum flavor before roasting until crispy. Together, with the creamy Caesar-style dressing and crunchy croutons, it's an irresistible combination.

serves 2

CRISPY BUTTER BEANS

1 (14-oz [400-g]) can butter beans, drained, rinsed and patted dry

¼ tsp salt

Black pepper, to taste

½ tsp dried sage

½ tsp dried thyme

1 tsp fresh lemon juice

1 tbsp (15 ml) olive oil

CROUTONS

1½ chunky slices of sourdough, cut into chunks

Salt and pepper, to taste

2 tsp (10 ml) olive oil

CAESAR-STYLE DRESSING

1 tbsp (15 ml) olive oil

2 tbsp (30 g) vegan mayonnaise

1 tsp capers, very finely chopped

2 tsp (10 ml) caper brine

2 tbsp (30 ml) fresh lemon juice

1 tbsp (3 g) nutritional yeast

4 cups (300 g) romaine lettuce, washed and roughly shredded

To make the beans: Preheat the oven to 425°F (220°C or gas mark 7). Line two baking trays with parchment paper.

Add the butter beans to a large bowl and season with the salt and a few grinds of black pepper. Add the sage, thyme, lemon juice and oil, and toss until the beans are well coated.

Spread the beans over the tray. Roast them for 20 minutes, until mostly crispy, shaking the tray halfway through to stir the beans.

Meanwhile, make the croutons: Add the chunks of bread to a lined baking tray and season with salt and pepper. Drizzle with the oil and stir until the bread is evenly coated. Roast at the same temperature as the beans for about 10 minutes, or until golden.

To make the dressing: Add the oil, vegan mayonnaise, capers, brine, lemon juice and nutritional yeast to a small bowl. Mix well to combine.

In a large bowl, toss the shredded lettuce with the roasted beans, croutons and some of the dressing. Add more dressing if needed. Once everything is evenly mixed, serve in two bowls with any extra dressing on the side.

edamame "sushi" salad with sesame soy dressing

If you're a sushi lover, this is the salad for you! Sushi is one of my favorite takeouts—I love the freshness and light but punchy flavor. Imagine all the fresh, vibrant flavors of sushi in one bowl: bright pickled ginger, creamy avocado, sticky rice, crunchy radish and refreshing cucumber all tossed together with an umami-packed dressing. If you like a bit of heat, mix some wasabi into the dressing for an added layer of warming flavor.

serves 2

DRESSING
1 tbsp (15 ml) sesame oil
1 tbsp (15 ml) soy sauce
1 tbsp (15 ml) rice wine vinegar
½ tsp wasabi (optional)
Heaped ½ cup (75 g) radish, finely sliced

SALAD
1 cup (250 g) cooked sushi or sticky rice
1 tbsp (15 ml) rice or sushi vinegar
1½ cups (225 g) frozen edamame, cooked
1 avocado, diced
⅓ cucumber, diced
2 spring onions, finely sliced
1½ tbsp (20 g) pickled sushi ginger, finely chopped

TOPPINGS
1 tbsp (9 g) sesame seeds
½ sheet of dried nori, cut into thin strips

To make the dressing: Mix together the oil, soy sauce, vinegar and wasabi (if using). Add the radish to the dressing and leave to one side to marinate while you prepare the rest of the salad.

To make the salad: Add the rice to a large mixing bowl. Pour in the vinegar and mix well. Use a fork to break up the rice. Add the edamame, avocado, cucumber, spring onions and pickled ginger to the large bowl with the rice. Mix to make sure everything is evenly distributed.

Add the dressing and marinated radish to the large bowl with the rice and mix well. Serve the salad in two bowls, topped with the sesame seeds and nori.

Note: Use dry scissors to cut the nori into thin strips.

charred lettuce wedges with Ranch-style Dressing & Beany "Bacon" Bits

Chargrilling vegetables is a lot of fun, and it gives the flavor a real boost. Both the lettuce and corn are charred in this salad, topped with beany "bacon" bits (inspired by those addictively crispy little morsels found in '90s salad bars) and finished with a drizzle of creamy ranch-style dressing.

serves 2 as a main or 4 as a side

BEANY "BACON" BITS

¾ cup (135 g) canned aduki or pinto beans, drained, rinsed & patted dry

1 tsp maple syrup

1 tsp olive oil

½ tsp smoked paprika

½ tsp tamari or soy sauce

¼ tsp salt

CHARRED CORN & LETTUCE

1 large corn cob, husk and silk removed

2 tsp (10 ml) neutral oil, divided

2 little gem lettuces, halved lengthways

RANCH DRESSING

2 tbsp (30 g) vegan mayonnaise

2 tbsp (30 g) plain, unsweetened vegan yogurt

1 tbsp (4 g) chopped fresh dill

1 tbsp (3 g) chopped fresh chives

¼ tsp onion granules

¼ tsp salt, plus more to taste

1 tbsp (15 ml) fresh lemon juice

Black pepper, to taste

To make the bacon bits: Preheat the oven to 425°F (220°C or gas mark 7) or air fryer to 350°F (180°C). If using the oven, line a baking tray with parchment paper.

Add the beans to a medium-sized bowl and toss them with the maple syrup, oil, smoked paprika, tamari and salt.

Spread the beans over the tray or add them to your air fryer basket. Oven roast for 15 minutes or air fry for 10 minutes, until crispy. Leave on the tray to cool.

Meanwhile, prepare the charred veg: Brush the corn with 1 teaspoon of the oil and cook on a hot griddle pan or grill until lightly charred, turning every minute or so to ensure even cooking. Brush the lettuce halves with the remaining 1 teaspoon of oil. Cook on the griddle pan/grill in the same way as the corn. Once cool enough to touch, use a sharp knife to carefully slice the corn kernels off the cob.

Make the dressing by combining the vegan mayonnaise, yogurt, herbs, onion granules, salt and lemon juice together in a small bowl. Season with salt and pepper to taste.

Arrange the charred lettuce on a large plate topped with the charred corn and beany "bacon" bits. Drizzle with the ranch dressing and serve any extra corn and beany "bacon" bits on the side.

Antipasti Bean Salad

The best thing about this salad is it uses almost all pantry ingredients, so it's easy to throw together—even when the fridge is empty! It makes a great addition to a sharing table or a tasty side for a barbecue. It's great when served immediately, but if you make it ahead of time, the beans have even longer to soak up all the delicious flavors. I personally think this salad is best the day after you make it, so plan ahead!

serves 2 as a main or 4 as a side

SALAD

2 (14-oz [400-g]) cans butter beans, drained and rinsed

Salt and pepper, to taste

⅓ cup (100 g) marinated artichoke hearts, finely chopped

½ cup (75 g) jarred sun-dried tomatoes, finely chopped

⅓ cup (75 g) pitted kalamata olives, finely chopped

½ cup (30 g) finely chopped fresh parsley

DRESSING

2 tbsp (30 ml) olive oil from the sun-dried tomato jar

1 tbsp (15 ml) extra virgin olive oil

1 tbsp (15 ml) red wine vinegar

½ tsp Dijon mustard

1 tsp dried oregano

1 tsp sugar or agave

1 tbsp (15 g) smoked almonds, roughly chopped, for garnish

To make the salad: Add the butter beans to a large bowl and season well with salt and pepper. Add the artichokes, sun-dried tomatoes, olives and parsley to the bowl. Toss everything together.

To make the dressing: Combine the oils, vinegar, mustard, oregano and sugar in a small bowl.

Pour the dressing into the bowl with the beans and mix everything together. Leave to sit for at least 1 to 2 minutes to soak up the flavors of the dressing before serving. Serve, topped with the almonds.

Miso & Lime Noodle Salad with Edamame

This nourishing salad is light, refreshing and full of zing. The dressing really doesn't hold back on flavor: Lime, miso and sesame come together with agave for sweetness to make a punchy dressing you'll keep going back to. Eat it chilled in the summer for a refreshingly vibrant lunch or light dinner.

Serves 2

SALAD

2 portions of whole wheat noodles, cooked and drained

1 cup (150 g) cooked edamame beans

½ cucumber, seeds removed and sliced into half moons

½ cup (75 g) radish, thinly sliced

2 spring onions, thinly sliced

DRESSING

2 tbsp (30 ml) fresh lime juice

1 tbsp (15 g) miso

1 tbsp (15 ml) agave or maple syrup

1 tsp sesame oil

GARNISHES

⅓ cup (50 g) roasted cashews

2 tsp (10 g) mixed sesame seeds

1 tbsp (3 g) chopped fresh cilantro

TO SERVE

Lime wedges

To make the salad: Add the noodles, edamame, cucumber, radish and spring onions to a large bowl and toss together. Set aside.

To make the dressing: Add the lime juice, miso, agave and oil to a small bowl. Mix well to combine.

Pour the dressing into the bowl with the noodles and toss well to coat everything.

Serve the salad in two bowls, topped with cashews, sesame seeds and cilantro with lime wedges on the side to squeeze over before eating.

zucchini, Broad Bean & mint salad with creamy Lemon Tofu

Broad beans can get a bad rep for being a bit bitter, but you don't need to worry about that in this recipe. They're marinated in the most vibrant, minty dressing to ensure maximum flavor without the bitterness. Chargrilled zucchinis sit on a bed of creamy, zesty whipped tofu topped with the marinated broad beans to create a gloriously green plate ready for you to tuck in.

serves 2 as a main or 4 as a side

SALAD
1 cup (150 g) frozen broad beans

1 medium zucchini, cut into ½-inch (1-cm) slices

2 tsp (10 ml) olive oil

DRESSING
½ cup (10 g) fresh mint leaves

2 tbsp (30 ml) olive oil

2 tbsp (30 ml) apple cider vinegar

½ tsp agave

¼ tsp salt

CREAMY LEMON TOFU
8 oz (220 g) firm tofu, drained

Zest of 1 lemon

2 tbsp (30 ml) fresh lemon juice, plus more to taste

2 cloves garlic

¼ tsp chile flakes

¼ tsp salt, plus more to taste

GARNISHES
Mint leaves

Lemon zest

Chile flakes

Flaked almonds, toasted

To prepare the beans: Add the beans to a medium-sized pan of lightly salted boiling water. Simmer for about 4 minutes, until tender. Rinse with cold water until the beans are cool to touch, then drain the beans. Shell the beans (if not already), rinse and drain again.

To make the dressing: Add the mint, oil, vinegar, agave and salt to a small blender, or a beaker if using an immersion blender. Blend until smooth. Add the cooled broad beans to the dressing and leave them to marinate.

To make the tofu: Add the tofu, lemon zest and juice, garlic, chile flakes and salt to a food processor. Blend until smooth and creamy, taste and add more salt or lemon juice if needed.

To make the salad: Brush the zucchini slices with the oil and cook them on a hot griddle pan or grill for 2 to 3 minutes on each side.

Spread the tofu over a serving plate. Top with the zucchini slices and spoon over the broad beans and mint dressing. Finish with mint leaves, lemon zest, chile flakes and toasted flaked almonds.

curried potato & Butter Bean salad

Potato salad is synonymous with barbecues in my family. Another barbecue classic is my mum's coronation chicken, and this dish is sort of a combination of the two. I love the contrast of the zingy pickled onions with the creamy, curried potatoes and butter beans. The dressing is pretty versatile and also works well on chickpeas as a tasty sandwich filling.

serves 2 as a main or 4 as a side

PINK PICKLED ONIONS

½ medium red onion, finely sliced

3 tbsp (45 ml) fresh lime juice

½ tbsp (3 g) finely chopped fresh mint

¼ tsp salt

½ tsp ground cumin

SALAD

2 cups (300 g) baby potatoes, halved or quartered

1 (14-oz [400-g]) can butter beans, drained and rinsed

Salt and pepper, to taste

DRESSING

3 tbsp (45 g) plain, unsweetened vegan yogurt

1 tbsp (15 ml) fresh lime juice

1½ tsp (3 g) medium curry powder

1½ tbsp (25 g) mango chutney

Zest of ½ lime

GARNISHES

Sliced green chile

Chopped fresh cilantro

Nigella seeds

To make the pickled onions: Add the onion to a small bowl and cover them with the lime juice. Add the mint, salt and cumin. Mix well and set aside while you prepare the rest of the salad ingredients.

To make the salad: Add the potatoes to a medium saucepan with salted boiling water. Simmer for 12 to 15 minutes, until fork-tender. Drain and leave to cool.

Add the butter beans to a large mixing bowl. Season well with salt and pepper.

To make the dressing: Combine the yogurt, lime juice, curry powder, chutney and lime zest in a small bowl. Add the potatoes to the bowl with the beans and pour in the dressing. Toss everything together until the beans and potatoes are well coated.

Serve the salad topped with green chile, cilantro and nigella seeds.

Smoky Bean Burrito Bowl with Chipotle Dressing

This is one of my all-time favorite meals: fiber-rich black beans, zingy tomato salsa, flavorsome cilantro (coriander) rice, punchy pickled onions and creamy avocado come together in one nutrient-dense bowl. It's a lot of fun to make and the flavors of each element work so well together. A vibrantly tasty bowl full of exciting textures, colors and tastes finished with a drizzle of creamy chipotle dressing that'll have you hooked!

serves 2

PINK PICKLED ONIONS
½ medium red onion, finely sliced
⅓ cup (80 ml) apple cider vinegar

TOMATO SALSA
¾ cup (120 g) cherry tomatoes, quartered
¼ tsp salt
1 spring onion, finely sliced
1 tbsp (15 ml) fresh lime juice
1 tbsp (3 g) chopped fresh cilantro

CILANTRO RICE
1 (8.5-oz [240-g]) pouch whole-grain rice, cooked
2 tbsp (6 g) chopped fresh cilantro
Zest of ½ lime
¼ tsp salt

To make the pickled onions: Add the onion to a small bowl and cover them with the vinegar. Leave to marinate while you prepare the rest of the bowl components.

To make the salsa: Add the quartered tomatoes to a medium-sized bowl and season with the salt. Add the spring onion, lime juice and cilantro. Mix well.

To make the rice: Mix the cooked rice with the cilantro, lime zest and salt.

(continued)

smoky Bean Burrito Bowl with chipotle Dressing (continued)

CHIPOTLE DRESSING

1 tsp chipotle paste

2 tbsp (30 g) plain, unsweetened vegan yogurt

1 tbsp (15 ml) fresh lime juice

½ tsp agave

SMOKY BEANS

1 (14-oz [400-g]) can black beans, reserve 2 tbsp (30 ml) of liquid and drain the rest

¼ tsp salt, plus more to taste

2 tbsp (30 g) tomato paste

½ tsp smoked paprika

½ tsp ground cumin

TO SERVE

1 avocado, sliced

1 (7-oz [200-g]) can sweet corn, drained

Chopped fresh cilantro

Chile flakes

Lime wedges

To make the dressing: Add the chipotle paste, yogurt, lime juice and agave to a small bowl. Mix together to combine.

To make the smoky beans: Add the beans to a medium-sized pan over medium-low heat along with 2 tablespoons (30 ml) of liquid from the can. Season with the salt, then add the tomato paste, smoked paprika and cumin. Stir over the heat until the beans are piping hot, adding a splash of water if needed. Season to taste.

Load up two bowls with the cilantro rice, tomato salsa, avocado, sweet corn, smoky beans and pickled onions. Drizzle with the chipotle dressing and top with cilantro, chile flakes and wedges of lime for squeezing.

Spiced Squash Salad With Herby Beans & Tahini-orange Dressing

Butternut squash is an underrated salad ingredient (and vegetable in general), often upstaged by the visually similar sweet potato. Squash retains a bit more bite when roasted and is much less sweet, which I love. In this recipe, I've spiced it with cinnamon and cumin to add extra layers of flavor. The roasted squash and cannellini beans are served with an herby quinoa, spiked with juicy jewels of pomegranate and finished with a creamy tahini-orange dressing.

serves 2

SPICED SQUASH

2 cups (400 g) butternut squash, cut into chunks

¼ tsp salt

1 tbsp (15 ml) olive oil

1 tsp ground cinnamon

1 tsp ground cumin

BEANS

1 (14-oz [400-g]) can cannellini beans, drained, rinsed and patted dry

¼ tsp salt

2 tsp (10 ml) olive oil

1 tsp dried dill

Zest of ½ orange

QUINOA

½ cup (100 g) quinoa

1½ cups (350 ml) vegetable broth (stock)

¾ cup (50 g) kale, shredded

½ loosely packed cup (20 g) fresh parsley, finely chopped

½ cup (80 g) pomegranate seeds

2 tsp (10 ml) extra virgin olive oil

1 tbsp (15 ml) fresh orange juice

To make the squash: Preheat the oven to 425°F (220°C or gas mark 7). Line a baking tray with parchment paper.

Arrange the butternut squash on the tray. Season with the salt and drizzle with the oil. Sprinkle with the cinnamon and cumin and toss to coat. Roast for 15 minutes.

Meanwhile, prepare the beans: Add the beans to a small bowl and toss them with the salt, oil, dill and zest. Add the beans to the tray with the squash and roast for 15 minutes, until the squash is soft and the beans are starting to crisp on the edges.

To make the quinoa: In a medium saucepan, cover the quinoa with the broth and bring it to a simmer. Simmer for 10 minutes, or until most of the liquid has been absorbed. Cover the pan with a lid and remove from the heat.

(continued)

Spiced Squash Salad With Herby Beans & Tahini-Orange Dressing (continued)

DRESSING
2 tbsp (30 ml) fresh orange juice
2 tbsp (30 ml) fresh lemon juice
3 tbsp (45 g) tahini

To make the dressing: Combine the orange juice, lemon juice and tahini in a small bowl.

Add the cooked quinoa to a large mixing bowl and fluff it up with a fork. Add the kale, parsley, pomegranate, oil and orange juice.

Serve the quinoa on plates and top with the roasted squash and beans. Finish with a drizzle of dressing.

Herby Pesto Bean Salad with Vine-Ripened Tomatoes

In this bright, fresh salad, leafy parsley and fragrant basil are blended into a flavorsome pesto-inspired dressing. Toss it through hearty butter beans and creamy cannellini beans with some crunchy red onion and juicy cherry tomatoes and you've got yourself a banging summery salad. The toasted pine nuts on top give a nice bit of crunch, but you can substitute them with any seeds or chopped nuts you fancy!

serves 2 as a main or 4 as a side

PESTO DRESSING

3 cups (60 g) fresh basil, divided

⅓ cup (15 g) fresh flat-leaf parsley

2 tbsp (6 g) nutritional yeast

2 tbsp (30 ml) extra virgin olive oil

1 tbsp (15 ml) fresh lemon juice, plus more to taste

Zest of ½ lemon

¼ tsp salt, plus more to taste

1 small clove garlic

SALAD

1 (14-oz [400-g]) can butter beans, drained and rinsed

1 (14-oz [400-g]) can cannellini beans, drained and rinsed

Salt and pepper, to taste

½ small red onion, thinly sliced

1⅓ cups (200 g) vine-ripened cherry tomatoes, halved or quartered depending on size

1 cup (20 g) arugula

3 tbsp (25 g) toasted pine nuts

To make the dressing: Add half of the basil, the parsley, nutritional yeast, oil, lemon juice and zest, salt and garlic to a blender, or beaker if using an immersion blender. Add 1 tablespoon (15 ml) of water and blend until mostly smooth. Then add the second half of the basil and blend again until smooth. Season to taste with more salt or lemon if needed.

To make the salad: Add the beans to a large bowl and season well with salt and pepper. Add the dressing and mix until the beans are well coated.

Add the onion and tomatoes, and mix through the beans. Once evenly distributed, add the arugula and stir it through. Top with toasted pine nuts just before serving.

edamame & mango salad with chile-lime dressing

This salad is inspired by the exciting Southeast Asian flavors of Thailand and Vietnam. There's crunch from the carrot, cucumber and peanuts, slight sweetness from the mango, creamy nuttiness from the edamame beans and fragrant herbs in abundance. Tossed together with a punchy dressing of lime juice, soy sauce and red chile, it's a bright and colorful salad that's bursting with flavor.

serves 2

SALAD

2 medium carrots, julienned or finely sliced into strips

2 tbsp (30 ml) rice vinegar

1 mango, peeled, pitted and sliced into strips

½ cucumber, seeds removed, cut into thin strips

1 cup (150 g) frozen edamame

½ cup (15 g) fresh cilantro, finely chopped

½ cup (15 g) fresh Thai basil, finely chopped

⅓ cup (10 g) fresh mint, finely chopped

2 tbsp (20 g) chopped roasted peanuts

DRESSING

1 tsp diced chile

1 clove garlic, minced

1½ tbsp (22 ml) light soy sauce

1½ tbsp (22 ml) fresh lime juice

½ tsp sugar

2 tbsp (30 ml) rice vinegar (from the carrots)

To make the salad: Add the carrots to a medium-sized bowl, cover them with the vinegar and leave to one side.

In another bowl, add the mango, cucumber, edamame and the herbs. Toss together.

To make the dressing: Add the chile, garlic, soy sauce, lime juice and sugar to a small bowl. Add the vinegar from the carrots and mix well.

Add the carrots and peanuts to the bowl with the mango, cucumber and herbs. Toss gently to mix everything together.

Pour in the dressing and mix again. Serve immediately.

Roasted Veg & Orzo Salad with Harissa Dressing

Pasta salad has been leveled up! The colorful veg becomes all kinds of sweet and charred after roasting, paired with creamy cannellini beans, orzo and a punchy harissa dressing to make a wonderfully tasty salad. It's also a brilliant one for prepping in advance and holds well in the fridge.

serves 2 as a main or 4 as a side

ROASTED VEG & ORZO

½ large red onion, cut into large slices

1 red bell pepper, roughly chopped into 1-inch (2.5-cm) pieces

1 cup (150 g) cherry tomatoes, halved

1 large zucchini, cut into ½-inch (1-cm) slices

½ tsp salt

1 tbsp (15 ml) olive oil, plus more for drizzling

1 cup (180 g) orzo

2½ cups (600 ml) vegetable broth (stock)

HARISSA DRESSING

1 tbsp (15 ml) extra virgin olive oil

2 tbsp (30 g) harissa

2 tbsp (30 ml) fresh lemon juice

2 tbsp (8 g) chopped fresh parsley

SALAD

1 (14-oz [400-g]) can cannellini beans, drained and rinsed

Salt and pepper, to taste

To make the veg: Preheat the oven to 425°F (220°C or gas mark 7).

Spread the vegetables over a large baking tray, or two smaller trays. Season with the salt and drizzle with oil. Stir on the tray to coat. Roast for about 20 minutes, or until everything is soft and starting to color on the edges.

Meanwhile, make the orzo: Add the orzo to a medium saucepan and cover it with the broth. Place the pan over medium heat and simmer for 10 to 15 minutes, or until al dente. Drain the cooked orzo, rinse with cold water and drain again. Drizzle with a little oil to prevent it from sticking together.

To make the dressing: Combine the oil, harissa, lemon juice and parsley in a small bowl.

To make the salad: In a large mixing bowl, toss the cooked orzo together with the roasted veg, cannellini beans and dressing. Season with salt and pepper to taste.

White Bean, Tomato & Dill Salad with Lemon Hummus Dressing

What started out as an experimental lunch one day has become a favorite salad that I keep coming back to time and time again. It's packed full of flavor and easy to whip up in only a couple of minutes. This salad seriously satisfies with cherry tomatoes, white beans and zucchini tossed in a creamy hummus dressing. The chile flakes and lemon add an extra zing that brings everything together for the perfect scrumptious bite.

Serves 2 as a main or 4 as a side

DRESSING

½ cup (120 g) hummus

1 tbsp (15 ml) fresh lemon juice

1 tbsp (15 ml) extra virgin olive oil

SALAD

1 (14-oz [400-g]) can cannellini beans, drained and rinsed

1 (14-oz [400-g]) can butter beans, drained and rinsed

Salt and pepper, to taste

Zest of 1 lemon

1 tbsp (15 ml) fresh lemon juice, plus more to taste

1 cup (130 g) zucchini, julienned or grated

1 cup (165 g) cherry tomatoes, quartered

½ cup (75 g) jarred sun-dried tomatoes, roughly chopped

½ cup (10 g) chopped fresh dill

1 tsp chile flakes

To make the dressing: Add the hummus, lemon juice and oil to a small bowl. Mix well to combine. Set aside.

To make the salad: Add the beans to a large bowl, and season them with salt and pepper. Add the lemon zest and juice. Mix well.

Use a sieve or muslin cloth to squeeze out any excess liquid from the grated zucchini. Add the zucchini, cherry tomatoes, sun-dried tomatoes, dill and chile flakes to the bowl with the beans. Stir through the dressing. Mix everything together and season with additional salt, pepper and lemon juice to taste.

Beany Snacks, Dips & Sides

If you know me, you'll know that I'm a serial snacker . . . so it's only right that there's a whole chapter dedicated to bean recipes that are perfect to munch on any time of the day (or night), as well as lots of delicious dips and tasty sides. Most of the recipes are super speedy and easy to prepare, such as the Smoky Barbecue Beans on Toast (page 128) and Bravas Beans with Garlic Aioli (page 117). They're great for throwing together when you're on your lunch break or short on time. Other recipes, such as the Crispy Spiced Potatoes on Garlicky Beans with Cilantro Chutney (page 125) or Black Bean Quesadillas with Cooling Avocado Sauce (page 135), take a bit more time—but they are so stunningly delicious you won't mind!

I hope these recipes give you inspiration for using beans in different ways. While they make excellent hero ingredients, they can take so many forms on the sidelines. I find myself making the Creamy Butter Bean & Mustard Mash (page 131) most weeks, as I never seem to have potatoes when I need them but there's almost always a can of butter beans in the cupboard. After you've read this book, I'm hoping you'll do the same!

I reckon dips are very underrated, especially as a snack option. High-protein snacks can help you feel fuller for longer and the beans in each recipe really help to pack in that protein and hopefully curb hunger pangs. The dips in this chapter are ridiculously easy to prepare, too. You just throw ingredients into a blender or food processor. Despite being straightforward to make, the flavors are complex and so delish. Serve them up with whatever you fancy for dipping: chips (crisps), oat cakes, crackers and vegetable crudités are some of my favorites. And they might be named "dips," but don't let that restrict you—they're brilliant as spreads on toast or sandwiches, too. Get creative!

Bravas Beans with Garlic Aioli

A play on the classic Spanish tapas dish, these beans will have you dreaming of sun-dappled streets and sangria. Smoked paprika brings a punchy, smoky flavor to the silky sauce while the garlicky aioli is ridiculously tempting—a plate of these won't last long!

Serves 4 as a Side

BRAVAS BEANS

3 tbsp (45 ml) olive oil

2 tsp (5 g) smoked paprika

2 tsp (5 g) all-purpose (plain) flour

½ cup (120 ml) vegetable broth (stock)

1 tbsp (15 g) tomato paste

2 (14-oz [400-g]) cans butter beans, drained and rinsed

Salt and pepper, to taste

VEGAN AIOLI

3 tbsp (45 g) vegan mayonnaise

1 tsp fresh lemon juice

2 cloves garlic

Pinch of salt

To make the beans: Whisk together the oil, smoked paprika and flour in a medium-sized pan. Put the pan over very low heat and stir continuously for about 3 minutes to cook out the raw flour taste.

In a jug or mug, mix the broth and the tomato paste using a fork or small whisk.

Make sure the pan with the oil, flour and paprika is over medium-low heat. Then pour in a small amount of the broth mixture. Whisk the contents of the pan until the sauce thickens before adding a little more broth. Repeat this until all the broth mixture is incorporated into the sauce and the sauce is smooth and glossy.

Add the butter beans to the pan and stir to make sure they're well coated. Season to taste with salt and pepper, then remove from the heat.

To make the aioli: Add the vegan mayonnaise, lemon juice, garlic and salt to a beaker and use an immersion blender to blend until smooth.

Serve the beans in a bowl topped with a drizzle of the aioli.

Butter Bean & Cauliflower Gratin

Cauliflower cheese is a classic British side dish and accompaniment to a traditional roast dinner that has now gained popularity pretty much the world over. My take uses beans (of course), both in the sauce and alongside the cauliflower, and is topped with golden breadcrumbs. Roasting the cauliflower is a flavor game-changer—the golden-edged, slightly nutty florets are just delicious. Pair them with hearty butter beans and coat everything in a tangy, "cheesy" yet creamy sauce and you have yourself a winner.

serves 4 as a side

CAULIFLOWER

5 cups (575 g) cauliflower, chopped into florets

½ tsp salt

2 tsp (10 ml) olive oil

1 (14-oz [400-g]) can butter beans, drained and rinsed

"CHEESY" SAUCE

1 (14-oz [400-g]) can cannellini beans, drained and rinsed

¼ cup (12 g) nutritional yeast

1 tsp garlic granules

1 tbsp (15 g) Dijon mustard

2 tsp (10 ml) apple cider vinegar

⅓ cup plus 1½ tbsp (100 ml) vegetable broth (stock)

⅓ cup plus 1½ tbsp (100 ml) unsweetened soymilk

Salt and pepper, to taste

BREADCRUMB TOPPING

⅓ cup (20 g) breadcrumbs

¼ tsp garlic granules

Pinch of salt

Preheat the oven to 400°F (200°C or gas mark 6).

Spread the cauliflower florets over a baking tray and season with the salt. Drizzle them with oil and stir on the tray to coat. Roast the cauliflower for about 20 minutes, until golden around the edges and soft throughout.

While the cauliflower is roasting, make the sauce: Add the cannellini beans, nutritional yeast, garlic granules, mustard, vinegar, broth and soymilk to a blender. Blend until smooth and creamy, then season with salt and pepper to taste.

Add the roasted cauliflower and the butter beans to an ovenproof dish. Pour the sauce over and gently mix until everything is evenly coated with sauce.

To make the topping: Combine the breadcrumbs, garlic granules and salt in a small bowl.

Cover the top of the cauliflower mix with breadcrumbs and roast for 15 to 20 minutes, or until bubbling and the breadcrumbs are golden and crispy. Serve immediately.

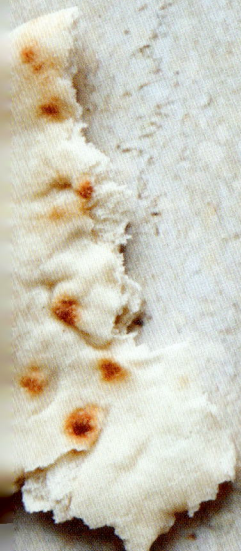

smoky kidney bean dip

This vibrant dip doesn't hold back on flavor! Hearty kidney beans are blended with roasted red peppers, punchy sun-dried tomatoes, garlic and smoked paprika to make a seriously flavorful dip with a satisfyingly smooth texture. It takes just minutes to prepare and uses mostly pantry ingredients—a perfect addition to a sharing board or lunch table.
I always like having it in the fridge to snack on or spread on toast.

serves 2

1 (14-oz [400-g]) can kidney beans, drained

⅔ cup (140 g) jarred roasted red peppers

⅓ cup (70 g) jarred sun-dried tomatoes

1 tbsp (15 ml) extra virgin olive oil

½ tsp garlic granules

½ tsp smoked paprika

1 tsp fresh lemon juice, plus more to taste

½ tsp salt, plus more to taste

Add the beans, peppers, sun-dried tomatoes, oil, garlic granules, smoked paprika, lemon juice and salt to a blender or food processor. Blend until as smooth as possible.

Season to taste with salt, and add additional lemon juice if needed.

Beany "Sausage" Rolls

Classic puff pastry sausage rolls have had a beany makeover! Mushrooms, kidney beans and black beans come together with miso and a few other ingredients to make the tastiest umami-packed filling. They're baked until flaky and golden and served up with sweet and sticky teriyaki sauce for dipping. Delish!

Makes about 26 rolls

"SAUSAGE" ROLLS

4 cups (300 g) chestnut mushrooms

¼ tsp salt

1 (14-oz [400-g]) can kidney beans, drained and rinsed

½ cup (90 g) canned black beans, drained and rinsed

2 tsp (3 g) onion granules

1 tbsp (15 g) miso

2 tbsp (30 ml) soy sauce

2 tbsp (14 g) breadcrumbs

1 (11.3-oz [320-g]) pre-rolled sheet of vegan puff pastry, at room temperature

To make the filling: Add the mushrooms to a food processor and pulse until they resemble a mince-like texture.

Add the mushrooms to a large, nonstick frying pan over medium heat and season with the salt. Cook over the heat for about 5 minutes, stirring now and again, until the moisture starts to release from the mushrooms. Cook for an additional 5 minutes, until the mushrooms have reduced in volume and the liquid has mostly evaporated. They should also be darker.

Add the cooked mushrooms back to the food processor with the kidney beans, black beans, onion granules, miso, soy sauce and breadcrumbs.

Pulse for a few seconds at a time until the mixture is mostly smooth, with a little bit of texture. You may need to use a spatula to scrape down the sides in between blending.

Preheat the oven to 425°F (220°C or gas mark 7). Line two baking trays with parchment paper.

Unroll the pastry sheet and place it on a clean, floured surface. Use a sharp knife to carefully slice the pastry in half lengthways. On the right-hand side of each piece of pastry, ¾ inch (2 cm) from the edge, spoon a long line of the mushroom/bean mixture from the top of the pastry to the bottom.

Carefully lift up the left-hand side of the pastry and fold it over the top of the mixture. Line it up with the right edge of the pastry. Use a fork to press down and seal the two edges together. Repeat with the other half of the pastry.

(continued)

Beany "sausage" Rolls (continued)

PASTRY GLAZE

1 tbsp (15 ml) tamari or soy sauce

1 tsp sesame oil

1 tsp black sesame seeds

1 tsp white sesame seeds

FOR SERVING

¼ cup (75 g) teriyaki sauce

Cut each long pastry sausage into 1½-inch (4-cm) pieces. Arrange the pieces onto the two large, lined baking trays, leaving plenty of space in between for the pastry to puff up.

To make the glaze: Mix the tamari and oil together in a small bowl. Using a pastry brush, lightly brush each roll all over with the glaze. Using a small, sharp knife, carefully cut two small slits on top of each roll. Sprinkle the rolls with sesame seeds.

Bake for about 20 to 25 minutes, until the pastry is flaky and golden. Serve the rolls with a dish of teriyaki sauce for dipping.

crispy spiced potatoes on garlicky Beans with cilantro chutney

Inspired by Indian flavors, these crispy roasted potatoes are coated in a tantalizing spice mix. The cooling garlicky bean puree is brightened with fragrant mint and is perfect for dunking the golden potatoes. The vibrant cilantro (coriander) chutney brings a whole other layer of exciting flavors: hot, sharp, sweet and punchy.

serves 2

CRISPY SPICED POTATOES

2 cups (450 g) baby potatoes, halved or quartered

¼ tsp salt

1 tbsp (15 ml) rapeseed oil

¼ tsp ground turmeric

1 tsp garam masala

GARLIC BEAN PUREE

1 (14-oz 400-g) can cannellini beans, drained and rinsed

⅓ cup (85 g test) plain, unsweetened vegan yogurt

2 cloves garlic

½ tsp salt

2 tbsp (11 g) chopped fresh mint

1 tbsp (15 ml) fresh lemon juice

To make the potatoes: Preheat the oven to 425°F (220°C or gas mark 7). Line a baking tray with parchment paper.

Add the potatoes to a large pot of salted boiling water. Boil them for about 12 minutes, or until soft enough for a knife to go into them without effort. Drain well and leave to steam dry for 1 to 2 minutes.

Either in the pot you boiled the potatoes in or a large bowl, toss the potatoes with the salt, oil, turmeric and garam masala. Spread them over the tray and roast them in the oven for 30 to 35 minutes, or until golden and crispy. Remove them from the oven.

While the potatoes are roasting, make the bean puree and cilantro chutney.

To make the puree: Add the cannellini beans to a blender or food processor along with the yogurt, garlic, salt, mint and lemon juice. Blend until smooth.

(continued)

Crispy spiced potatoes on garlicky beans with cilantro chutney (continued)

CILANTRO CHUTNEY

1 cup (35 g) fresh cilantro (coriander)

1 clove garlic

1 tsp ground cumin

1 green chile

2 tsp (10 ml) fresh lemon juice

¼ tsp salt

Pinch of sugar or a dash of agave

GARNISHES

1 tsp chile flakes

1 tbsp (9 g) crushed roasted peanuts

To make the chutney: Add the cilantro, garlic, cumin, green chile, lemon juice, salt and sugar to a small blender or beaker if using an immersion blender. Add a splash of water if needed to blend. Blend until smooth.

Spread the garlicky beans over a large plate. Top with the crispy potatoes and drizzle with the chutney. Finish with a sprinkle of chile flakes and the crushed peanuts.

smoky Barbecue Beans on Toast

A beans cookbook just wouldn't be complete without a recipe for beans on toast, would it?! You might have already gathered I'm a big fan of beans, but canned baked beans are the only exception—there's something about the texture of the sauce that I just can't get on board with (crazy, I know!). I've been on a mission to nail the perfect beans on toast, and I think this could well be the one. The sauce is slightly sweet, smoky, warming, tangy and so delicious. Feel free to add a few dashes of tabasco for extra heat.

serves 2

BARBECUE BEANS
2 tsp (10 ml) olive oil
½ medium red onion, finely sliced
1 (14-oz [400-g]) can haricot beans
1½ (3 g) tsp smoked paprika
¼ tsp salt
½ tsp chile flakes
⅔ cup (160 ml) passata
1 tsp balsamic vinegar
1 tsp tamari or dark soy sauce
1½ (7 ml) tsp maple syrup

TOAST
2 slices of sourdough bread
1 tbsp (15 g) vegan butter

GARNISH
1 tsp chile flakes
1 tbsp (3 g) chopped fresh chives

To make the beans: Add the oil and onion to a medium-sized pan. Fry over medium heat for a few minutes, until soft and almost golden. Set the heat to medium-low.

Reserve 1 tablespoon (15 ml) of liquid from the can before draining and rinsing the beans. Add the drained and rinsed beans, the reserved liquid, the smoked paprika and the salt to the pan and stir for a minute.

Add the chile flakes, passata, vinegar, tamari and maple syrup. Mix well and stir over the heat for at least 10 minutes, until the sauce has reduced and is coating the beans.

Once reduced, toast your bread and spread with butter. Serve the beans on the buttered toast with a sprinkle of chile flakes and chives.

creamy Butter Bean & Mustard Mash

I'm not going to try to tell you that mashed potatoes aren't delicious—I'd be wasting my time. Nonetheless, this butter bean mash is a seriously tasty, protein-packed alternative. It's ridiculously creamy and so comforting—I don't think there's been a time when I haven't eaten some straight out of the pan. I love to finish it with a good crack of black pepper and top with a bit of extra butter.

serves 2 as a side

2 (14-oz [400-g]) cans butter beans, drained and rinsed

1 tbsp (15 g) whole-grain mustard

1 tsp Dijon mustard

1 tsp garlic granules

½ cup (120 ml) unsweetened soymilk, plus more as needed

½ tsp salt, plus more to taste

1 tbsp (15 g) vegan butter, plus more for serving

Black pepper, to taste

1 tbsp (4 g) chopped fresh parsley, to garnish (optional)

Add the beans, mustards, garlic granules, soymilk and salt to a food processor. Blend until smooth.

Once smooth, add the mash to a medium-sized pan over low heat and stir for a few minutes, until piping hot throughout.

Add the butter to the mash in the pan, and stir gently until melted and mixed through.

Add a splash more milk, if needed, to reach your desired consistency and season to taste with salt and pepper.

Serve immediately, topped with parsley and a little more vegan butter, if desired.

White Bean Hash Browns with Jammy Tomatoes

Hash browns are always a crowd-pleaser, and these butter bean and potato ones are no exception. They can be baked in the oven, or in the air fryer for extra crispness. If you're wondering where the jammy tomatoes come in, think ketchup but with ten times more flavor. Hopefully these will become a regular in your savory brunch repertoire!

Makes 6 to 8 hash browns

HASH BROWNS
2 medium potatoes, grated
1 (14-oz [400-g]) can butter beans, drained and rinsed
½ large yellow (brown) onion, grated
½ tsp garlic granules
¾ tsp salt
Black pepper, to taste
1 tbsp (15 ml) olive oil

To make the hash browns: Preheat the oven to 400°F (200°C or gas mark 6) or the air fryer to 350°F (180°C). If using the oven, line a baking tray with parchment paper.

Squeeze the liquid out of the potatoes and collect it in a small bowl. Set it side.

In a large, shallow bowl, mash the butter beans with a fork or potato masher. Add the potatoes, onion, garlic granules, salt and a few grinds of black pepper.

The starch in the liquid from potatoes should have separated and sunk to the bottom of the bowl. Carefully spoon out the excess liquid and discard, leaving the white starch behind. Add it to the bowl with the beans, onion and potatoes and mix well.

Use your hands to shape the mix into rounds about 3 inches (8 cm) in diameter and ½ inch (just over 1 cm) thick.

Brush one side of the hash browns with oil and place them oiled side down on the tray or into your air fryer basket. Brush the top side with oil.

Roast in the oven for about 40 minutes, or air fry for 20 to 25 minutes, turning halfway through, until the hash browns are golden on the outside and the potatoes and onion are cooked through.

(continued)

White Bean Hash Browns with Jammy Tomatoes (continued)

JAMMY TOMATOES

1 cup (150 g) vine-ripened cherry tomatoes

½ tsp olive oil

¼ tsp salt

1 tsp balsamic vinegar

1 tsp agave

While the hash browns are cooking, make the jammy tomatoes: Add the tomatoes to a small pan with the oil and salt. Cook over medium heat for 5 minutes, stirring now and again, while they blister and start to soften. After 5 minutes, start to smoosh them down with the back of a spoon.

Add the vinegar and agave and mix well. Stir over medium heat for 3 to 5 minutes to reduce. Blend with an immersion blender until smooth.

Serve the hash browns with a bowl of jammy tomatoes alongside for dipping.

Black Bean Quesadillas with Cooling Avocado Sauce

Who doesn't love a quesadilla?! Black beans are cooked with jalapeños, smoked paprika, chile and cumin to make the easy—and delicious—filling. Stuffed into wraps and topped with a "cheesy" bean-based sauce, they're baked until crisp and served with a cooling avocado sauce for dipping.

Makes about 9 quesadillas

BLACK BEAN & JALAPEÑO FILLING

2 (14-oz [400-g]) cans black beans, reserve ¼ cup (60 ml) liquid and drain the rest

2 tbsp (30 g) finely chopped jarred jalapeños

½ tsp smoked paprika

½ tsp ground cumin

½ tsp chile flakes

3 tbsp (45 g) tomato paste

1 tsp soy sauce

Salt and pepper, to taste

"CHEESY" SAUCE

⅔ cup (120 g) canned cannellini beans, drained and rinsed

⅓ cup (80 ml) unsweetened soymilk

¼ cup (20 g) nutritional yeast

¼ tsp garlic granules

½ tsp salt, plus more if needed

1 tsp apple cider vinegar or fresh lemon juice, plus more if needed

To make the filling: Preheat the oven to 350°F (180°C or gas mark 4).

Add the black beans to a medium-sized pan along with ¼ cup (60 ml) of liquid, the jalapeños, smoked paprika, cumin, chile flakes, tomato paste and soy sauce. Mix well to make sure the beans are well coated and stir over medium-low heat until everything is heated through. Season to taste with salt and pepper and set aside.

To make the sauce: Add the cannellini beans, soymilk, nutritional yeast, garlic granules, salt and vinegar to a small blender or beaker if using an immersion blender. Blend until smooth. Add more vinegar and salt to taste.

(continued)

Black Bean Quesadillas
with Cooling Avocado Sauce (continued)

QUESADILLAS

9 small flour tortillas or soft taco wraps

2 spring onions, finely sliced

1 tbsp (15 ml) olive oil

AVOCADO SAUCE

½ avocado

½ tsp garlic granules

½ tsp salt, plus more to taste

⅓ cup (85 g) plain, unsweetened vegan yogurt

Packed ⅓ cup (20 g) fresh cilantro

2 tsp (10 ml) fresh lime juice

Black pepper, to taste

To make the quesadillas: Lay the wraps flat and cover half with about 2 tablespoons (20 g) of the bean mixture. Spread 1 tablespoon (15 ml) of the "cheesy" sauce on top of the beans and add a sprinkle of spring onion.

Fold the wraps in half to cover the filling. Brush the outside of the wraps with a little oil and spread them out over two oven trays. Bake for 10 to 15 minutes, until the wraps are lightly golden.

While the wraps are baking, make the avocado sauce: Add the avocado, garlic granules, salt, yogurt, cilantro and lime juice to a blender or food processor. Blend until smooth. Season to taste with salt and pepper.

Serve the quesadillas with a bowl of the avocado sauce on the side.

Lemon & Cilantro Bean Hummus with Olive & Cumin Oil

Hummus is arguably one of the most popular legume-based dips you can get. This recipe is fully inspired by it and uses cannellini beans in place of chickpeas for a creamy, silky-smooth finish. They're blended up with tahini, a squeeze of lemon and plenty of fresh cilantro for a light and zesty dip that really delivers on flavor. If you've never tried a flavored oil with your hummus, this one is a great way to start. It adds an extra layer of interest and really dials up the flavor. I think you'll love it!

serves 2

HUMMUS

1 (14-oz [400-g]) can cannellini beans, reserve 1 tbsp (15 ml) of liquid and drain the rest

1 tbsp (15 g) tahini

Zest of 1 lemon

2 tbsp (30 ml) fresh lemon juice, plus more if needed

½ tsp salt, plus more if needed

½ cup (10 g) fresh cilantro leaves

OLIVE & CUMIN OIL

1½ tbsp (22 ml) extra virgin olive oil

½ tsp ground cumin

5 kalamata olives, finely chopped

GARNISH

Fresh cilantro

To make the hummus: Add the cannellini beans plus 1 tablespoon (15 ml) of liquid, tahini, lemon zest and juice, and the salt to a food processor. Blend until mostly smooth. Add 1 ice cube and blend again until super smooth and creamy. If the hummus is too thick, add another ice cube. Add the cilantro and pulse until it is evenly mixed through the dip. Season to taste with more salt and/or lemon juice.

To make the olive and cumin oil: Add the oil and cumin to a small bowl and stir to combine. Add the olives and stir again.

Spread the hummus over a plate and drizzle with the oil. Finish with a sprinkle of cilantro.

whipped edamame & tofu dip with crispy soy mushrooms

As soon as you make this dip, you'll be wishing you tried it sooner! Edamame, silken tofu and avocado come together to make a light and creamy dip with so much flavor. It's a powerhouse of nutrients too, loaded with protein from the edamame and tofu as well as healthy fats from the avocado. Grab some crunchy crudités, some toasted bread or your favorite crisps, and get dipping! If you're lucky enough to have any left over, it makes for a delicious sandwich spread.

serves 2

WHIPPED EDAMAME & TOFU

¾ cup (125 g) cooked edamame

½ cup (130 g) silken tofu

½ avocado

1 clove garlic

2 tsp (10 ml) light soy sauce or tamari

½ tsp salt

1 tbsp (3 g) chopped fresh cilantro

Zest of 1 lime

2 tbsp (30 ml) fresh lime juice

CRISPY SOY MUSHROOMS

1 tsp sesame oil

1 cup (75 g) shiitake mushrooms, sliced

1 tsp soy sauce

GARNISHES

Chile flakes

Sesame seeds

Toasted sesame oil

To make the whipped edamame and tofu: Add the edamame, silken tofu, avocado, garlic, soy sauce, salt, cilantro and lime zest and juice to a blender or food processor. Pulse for a few seconds at a time, using a spatula to scrape down the edges if necessary. Continue until the consistency is smooth and creamy.

To make the mushrooms: Add the oil to a medium-sized pan over medium heat. Add the mushrooms and leave to crisp on one side for at least a couple of minutes before moving. Stir them a little, then let the other side crisp for a minute or so.

Once the mushrooms are mostly golden, add the soy sauce, stir and allow them to sizzle. Once golden and crispy on some edges, remove the mushrooms from the pan and spread them over a paper towel.

Spread the edamame mixture over a plate and top with the crispy mushrooms. Finish with a sprinkle of chile flakes and sesame seeds and a little drizzle of toasted sesame oil.

Herby Zucchini & Bean Fritters with Garlic Yogurt

Dill is one of my favorite herbs, and it plays a massive part in these herbaceous zucchini and bean fritters. Along with mint, the chopped dill is combined with the zucchini and cannellini bean mixture and pan-fried to form little golden fritters that are packed with flavor at every bite.

Makes about 14 to 16 fritters

HERBY ZUCCHINI & BEAN FRITTERS

1 (14-oz [400-g]) can cannellini beans, drained and rinsed

¾ tsp salt

1 medium zucchini, grated (1⅓ cups [230 g])

¼ cup (12 g) fresh dill, finely chopped

¼ cup (20 g) fresh mint leaves, finely chopped

⅔ cup (85 g) all-purpose (plain) flour

2 tbsp (14 g) breadcrumbs

2–3 tbsp (30–45 ml) neutral oil, for frying, divided

GARLIC YOGURT

¾ cup (175 g) plain, unsweetened vegan yogurt

1 large clove garlic

¼ tsp salt

HERB OIL

1 tbsp (15 ml) extra virgin olive oil

1 tbsp (4 g) chopped fresh parsley or dill, or both

Zest of ½ lemon

To make the fritters: Make sure the beans are well drained. Add them to a large bowl and mash with a fork or potato masher. Season them with the salt.

Add the zucchini, herbs, flour and breadcrumbs to the bowl. Mix well to combine everything. Scoop out 1 tablespoon (about 15 g) of the mixture and shape it into a round, flat fritter shape. Repeat until all the mixture is used up.

Add 1 tablespoon (15 ml) of the oil to a large, nonstick pan. Put the pan over medium heat and add some of the fritters, leaving enough space between them to turn. Cook for 2 minutes on the first side before carefully turning. Cook for 2 minutes on the other side. Repeat until both sides are golden. The fritters may become slightly soft as they fry, so be careful turning and removing them from the pan. They will firm up again as they cool. Add an additional tablespoon (15 ml) of the oil to the pan and cook the rest of the fritters as before. Depending on the size of your pan, you may need to cook the fritters in three batches rather than two; in that case, cook the final batch in 1 additional tablespoon (15 ml) of oil.

Once all the fritters are cooked, make the garlic yogurt and herb oil: Combine the yogurt, garlic and salt in a bowl.

To make the herb oil: In a small bowl, mix the oil with the herbs and lemon zest. Drizzle the oil over the yogurt and serve it alongside the fritters.

edamame, pea & lime spread

This edamame, cilantro and lime spread is a great alternative to smashed avocado and is delicious for breakfast, lunch, brunch or a savory snack spread on your favorite bread or toast. Edamame and peas have a brilliantly green color, and they're also packed with plant-based protein and fiber. If dips are more your thing, I love serving with some rice crackers for scooping up this zesty spread.

serves 2

SPREAD

¾ cup (125 g) frozen edamame, cooked and cooled

1 cup (125 g) frozen peas, cooked and cooled

2 tbsp (30 ml) fresh lime juice, plus more to taste

Zest of 1 lime

1 tsp sesame oil

½ tsp salt, plus more to taste

TO SERVE

Bread or toast for spreading, or crackers or crudités for dipping

GARNISHES

Sesame seeds

Chile flakes

Chopped fresh cilantro

To make the spread: Add the edamame, peas, lime juice and zest, oil and salt to a blender or food processor. Pulse until it is blended together but still has some texture. Season to taste with more lime juice or salt if needed.

Spread this on toast or serve it in a bowl for dipping. Top with a sprinkle of sesame seeds, chile flakes and cilantro.

sweet corn & Black Bean fritters with zesty salsa

These tasty fritters can be eaten hot or cold. They're a ridiculously tasty snack and make a great addition to lunch boxes. I've been known to eat the whole lot in one go . . . there's just something incredibly addictive about them, especially when topped with a dollop of fresh, zesty salsa.

Makes about 5 to 6 fritters

SWEET CORN & BLACK BEAN FRITTERS

1 cup (180 g) canned black beans, drained and rinsed

1¼ cups (200 g) canned sweet corn, drained

½ tsp salt

2 tsp (5 g) onion granules

1 tsp chile flakes

1 tbsp (3 g) chopped fresh cilantro

2 tbsp (16 g) all-purpose (plain) flour

2 tbsp (30 ml) neutral oil, for frying, divided

ZESTY SALSA

¾ cup (110 g) cherry tomatoes, quartered

¼ tsp salt, plus more to taste

1 tbsp (3 g) chopped fresh cilantro

1 spring onion, finely sliced

Zest of ½ lime

1 tbsp (15 ml) fresh lime juice, plus more to taste

To make the fritters: Add the black beans and corn to a large, shallow bowl. Use a fork or potato masher to roughly mash. Season with the salt, then add the onion granules, chile flakes and cilantro. Mix well.

Stir in the flour. Use your hands to shape the mixture into evenly sized patties.

Add half of the oil to a medium-sized, nonstick frying pan over medium heat. Once the oil is sizzling hot, add a few of the fritters to the pan, enough to fill it but leaving enough room to easily turn each.

Fry for about 2 minutes on the first side. Carefully turn using a spatula, then fry for 2 minutes on the other side. Repeat this for a minute at a time until the fritters are golden on both sides and cooked through. They will continue to harden up when cooling.

Add the rest of the oil to the pan and repeat as before until all the fritters are cooked.

To make the salsa: Add the cherry tomatoes, salt, cilantro, spring onion, and lime zest and juice to a bowl. Mix everything together, and season to taste with more salt and/or lime juice.

Serve the fritters with the bowl of salsa on the side to spoon on.

spiced crispy Bean snack Mixes

If you haven't been convinced already, beans are seriously versatile! Switch up your savory snack game and try roasting some with herbs and spices to make a deliciously crunchy mix to graze on. Any leftover crumbs and seasoning on the baking tray can be used as a sprinkle on salads, soups or roasted vegetables. The snacks themselves are also great garnishes—I love topping the Edamame, Coconut & Cilantro Soup (page 43) with the sesame soy black beans and the Turmeric Beans with Cumin Roasted Cauliflower (page 75) with a sprinkle of the spiced kidney beans.

Each mix serves 2 to 3

SMOKED PAPRIKA & GARLIC BUTTER BEANS

1 (14-oz [400-g]) can butter beans, drained and rinsed

2 tbsp (30 ml) extra virgin olive oil

2 tsp (4 g) garlic granules

2 tsp (2 g) dried rosemary

1 tsp salt

SESAME SOY BLACK BEANS

1 (14-oz [400-g]) can black beans, drained and rinsed

1 tbsp (15 ml) sesame oil

1 tbsp (15 ml) tamari or soy sauce

1 tbsp (9 g) sesame seeds

½ tsp chile flakes

SPICED KIDNEY BEANS

1 (14-oz [400-g]) can kidney beans, drained and rinsed

1 tbsp (15 ml) extra virgin olive oil

1 tsp salt

1 tsp maple syrup

1 tsp ground cumin

½ tsp chili powder

For each mix, preheat the oven to 425ºF (220ºC or gas mark 7).

For each mix, add all the ingredients to a large bowl. Mix until the beans are well coated. Spread them over a lined baking tray and roast for 20 to 25 minutes, or until crispy. They should crisp up a little more as they cool.

Leave on the tray to cool, then serve in bowls.

Acknowledgments

I am so grateful for the opportunity to write this book and wouldn't be here without the incredible support of my followers and online community. My biggest thank-you goes to all of you: for engaging with my content, sharing recipes with family and friends and posting pictures or sending messages when you try a recipe of mine. Your support encourages and motivates me on a daily basis to keep creating recipes.

I need to say a huge thank-you to all the incredible creators I've met (virtually and in-person) on this crazy journey. I feel so lucky to have made friendships and created memories that will last a lifetime. It's so amazing (and sometimes surreal) to meet people that you have so much in common with that it feels as if you've known them forever. Working online can be a lonely job, but having "colleagues" to share ups and downs with, turn to for advice and have open conversations with makes it a whole lot easier. Thank you for inspiring, supporting and collaborating with me.

A huge thank-you goes to my mum and dad, for believing in me, supporting me in everything I've ever done and giving me the advice and encouragement needed to follow my dreams. Thank you for inspiring my passion for food, teaching me to cook and bringing up the three of us to be hardworking, creative and adventurous in our own ways.

Thank you to my wonderful husband for being my biggest cheerleader and hype-man when I need it most. For always being excited to try my recipes and not so excited about the washing up. You've been by my side every step of the way, and I wouldn't be here without you.

To all of my family and friends, I feel incredibly grateful to have such a strong support network. Thank you for encouraging me, embracing my dietary requirements, sharing my recipes, sampling my creations and championing my work. There's always a (bean-filled) meal with your name on it.

Lastly, thank you to my editor, Sadie, designer, Laura, and the whole Page Street Publishing team for giving me this incredible opportunity, supporting me and making this book come to life. You've made one of my biggest dreams a reality, and I couldn't be more thankful.

About the Author

Sarah is a plant-based recipe developer and photographer. Through her food blog, (www.sarahsveganrecipes.com) and Instagram (@sarahsveganrecipes), she shares vibrant plant-based recipes with big flavor. Her goal is to prove that vegan food is far from boring and to encourage others to enjoy delicious plant-based meals through her easy-to-follow recipes. She loves to champion the versatility of vegetables, pulses and legumes, turning them into colorful, exciting dishes with all kinds of flavor.

Born and raised in Scotland, Sarah has spent the last five years living in London with her husband. When Sarah is not developing recipes or photographing food, she loves exploring London's incredible food scene: working her way through an ever-growing must-try list of bakeries, markets, restaurants and eateries. She loves traveling, exploring new countries, sampling the local cuisine and gathering recipe inspiration.

index